The Lost God of Christ: Resurrecting the Truth

This book is dedicated to all the courageous individuals, beginning with the carpenter from Nazarene, who have chosen to defend truth over tradition to the peril of life and limb.

The Forest through the Trees

My conscience is clear, but that doesn't prove I'm right. It is the Lord himself who will examine me and decide.

1st Corinthians 4:4

Sometime after I began writing this book an unusual event occurred. A search which began over thirty years ago for a long lost Leonardo Da Vinci fresco seemed to have actually yielded results. The fresco, known as *The Battle of Anghiari*, had been considered lost to time or destruction to all but the most determined treasure hunters.

Enter Professor Maurizio Seracini.

After being contacted by Da Vinci expert Carlo Pedretti in the 1970's Seracini began his quest to uncover the missing fresco. All evidence pointed to the possibility of the fresco lying safe and sound amidst other fantastic masterpieces in the Palazzo Vecchio.

The catch? (There's always a catch.)

It's believed to be buried under the present sight of the 16th century fresco, *The Battle of Marciano in Val di Chiana*, by Giorgio Vasari. During a recent restoration project on Vasari's fresco an air gap of between 10 and 15mm was found behind the wall. It is possible that Vasari built a façade over Da Vinci's fresco to preserve it for posterity; apparently, he had made similar efforts of this nature in the past in order to preserve other works of art.

The hook? (There's always a hook.)

Vasari's fresco contains the biblical words *Cerca Trova*: "seek and ye shall find." Perhaps this is the X

Seracini has been searching for all these years. Incidentally, if the name Seracini seems familiar it's because he is one of the few living persons that Dan Brown referenced in *The Da Vinci Code*.

Much like Seracini's hunt for the lost Da Vinci fresco, my goal in writing this book was to try to get under modern Christianity and shed some light on the true message of Jesus buried beneath it. I want to chisel through its various manmade doctrines to uncover the early church; and what I mean by "the early church" are the religious practices of Christ's disciples in the first decades following Christ's resurrection, and, perhaps more importantly, before Christianity became the politically expedient path to power and fortune in the Roman Empire.

Unfortunately for Seracini his efforts were shut down before he could ascertain its existence for fear of damaging Vasari's painting.

This is understandable.

Vasari's fresco is well preserved, and for it to be requisitioned in the first place the Da Vinci fresco must have been in extremely poor condition. This is actually believed to be the case as Da Vinci was known to have experimented unsuccessfully with pigments and painting style on this fresco. The painting in all probability faded before his very eyes.

Such is life.

However, to say that early Christianity needed a makeover because the original message of Christ faded or was unsuccessful in some way is to discredit Jesus Christ himself. His pure message of loving God and each other didn't deserve or require the cover-up it has received. Many of the rituals performed in churches each and every

Sunday for centuries have absolutely no connection with Christ's teachings. Rather, they have been interjected into his message over the millennia for a variety of reasons, both benign and malevolent. Thus, my aim is to clean the proverbial slate and get to the basics of Christianity; and in the process reveal what was actually founded in scripture, while exposing false teachings for what they are. While the primary goal is restoring God to the forefront of Christianity, the plan along the way is to also expose certain doctrines for what they are: unscriptural fabrications.

Much of what I address will be sore points for Christians who have been engulfed in modern Christianity; many of whom will undoubtedly shrug off this book before giving it a fair shake. The old adage of not talking religion and politics at gatherings is for good reason: changing the mind of someone who has already taken a side is all but a futile endeavor – and a waste of breath. Taking this into consideration, this book was written for the un-indoctrinated; for those who are brave enough to question the status quo; for those who aren't afraid of finding truth, even if it conflicts with one's very core beliefs.

To those whose doors of possibilities are held ajar ever so gently by the shoe of open-mindedness: good for you! My suggestion is to reference your Bible at every turn of the page. The points made within this book, while obvious, are not popular. It would be quite easy to dismiss them without ever giving them adequate time for proper discernment. That's why I implore you to read the scriptures first hand from your own Bible. If at the end you remain unmoved, so be it. I commend your openness to new possibilities and willingness to hear differing ideas, nonetheless.

1 No man is an Island

This great dragon—the ancient serpent called the devil, or Satan, the one deceiving the whole world—was thrown down to the earth with all his angels. Revelation 12:9

I once asked Mark, a great friend of mine who also happened to be a pastor, that if he were placed on a deserted island, with only the Holy Bible, would he come to the conclusion of the Holy Trinity (also known as the Godhead or Triune) on his own? We had been discussing its validity on and off for months, each of us quoting different sources and books from the past. To Mark, a firm believer of the concept, my sources were unreliable, and my newness to organized religion meant I just didn't understand; to me, Mark was dogmatic, regurgitating what he was taught without being open to new ideas.

Now to be fair there probably isn't a more honest, understanding, and open-minded pastor on the face of the earth than Mark. If there is anyone that could have been called dogmatic it's me. And to be even fairer, what I was asking Mark to do was to go against everything in which he was taught to believe from childhood, right up to through Bible college; namely, that the concept of the Trinity is a fact. This is what the vast majority of Christians have been taught to believe, clergy and congregations alike.

The problem is it's just not biblical.

At least this is the conclusion I was forming. It seemed to me every scripture I read pointed to a distinct hierarchy between God the Father, and his son Jesus. To make matters worse compared to God and Jesus the holy spirit hardly gets mentioned, and when it is it's rarely personified. It just didn't pan out. So I began to point out the contradictions and inconsistencies that occur within the Bible when the Trinity is assumed to be true. He quickly mentioned that the word Trinity isn't found anywhere in the Bible; he assured me, however, that the doctrine was based on scripture. He then quoted the usual few scriptures that are used to give credibility to which he undeniable admitted, amounts to a very complex concept. He cited: John 1:1, *"the word was God;"* John 10:38, *"the Father is in Me, and I in Him;"* John 10:30, *"I and My Father are one;"* Matthew 28:19, *"baptizing them in the name of the Father and of the Son and of the Holy Ghost;"* and, of course, 1st John 5:7, *"for there are three that bear record in heaven: the Father, the Word, and the Holy Ghost: and these three are one."*[1] Thus began our protracted discussion on the subject.

Now, Pastor Mark is a voracious reader of Christian books, and loves to recommend (and buy) books for his friends, and for members of the congregation. So, of course, he suggested reading material on the topic. It was about here that I realized that the majority of material used to "prove" the Trinity was merely the opinions of some, not-so-early theologians, writing long after the death of Jesus and his Apostles. These men attempted to marry the prevalent beliefs of their time, which included the philosophy of the Greeks, along with their pantheon of pagan gods and rituals, with Christianity. On the other hand, there were as many or more theologians of the same era who wrote against the concept of the Trinity. The differing opinions had each, in fact, vacillated between heretical and orthodox for centuries, depending on the church leader in power. Now considered heretical by the established Church, the writings of the opponents of the doctrine of the Trinity have largely been ignored or dismissed by most modern theologians of major Christian denominations. Tradition has the benefit of doubt; so whenever I mentioned these men to Pastor Mark he politely referred to writers in his school of thought as the only authorities on the subject.

To Mark, and the other Trinitarians with whom I spoke about the subject, I just didn't get it. More than once, I was given a condescending smile, and told that the Holy Trinity was either too complex for me to grasp, or that it was simply a matter of faith-faith that I obviously didn't have. They assured me though that in time I too would grow to understand, and appreciate the doctrine to be fact provided my faith grew.

One thing that I had already come to appreciate was that, with the very few exceptions given above, seldom did anyone use scripture to explain to me the existence of the Trinity. I was beginning to wonder the reason for this glaring void. I also began to realize that whenever I mentioned a scripture that refuted the concept of equality among the three parts of the Trinity, I was given a protracted explanation of what the scripture "really meant." It seemed that they were never taken at face value. This was puzzling. Why would God bother to give us a guidebook for life that was too complex for the average person to understand? Why have so many so-called scholars and theologians come between God's message and us? Didn't Jesus continually speak against the Priests and religious scholars of his time?

Pastor Mark and I were going around in circles. The more I read the Bible and writings of the early church fathers, the more I realized that I was only hearing men's interpretations of the Bible, particularly of its perspective regarding the Trinity doctrine. These interpretations quite often reflected both the religious and political whims of the day more than a factual understanding of scripture. Why would we need someone else to interpret what was intended to be easily understood by all men? After all, Christ and his followers spoke primarily to the common masses; the poor; the salt of the earth. How complicated could his message have been? Paul emphasized the simplicity of the message to the church in Corinth:

> *Christ [sent me]... to preach the Good News—and not with clever speech, for fear that the cross of Christ would lose its power... And my message and my preaching were very plain. Rather than using clever and persuasive speeches, I relied only on the power of the Holy Spirit. I did this so you would trust not in human wisdom but in the power of God [the Holy Spirit].* 1st Corinthians 1:17; 2:4-5

It was also around this time when, in my search for the truth, the idea of using scripture to prove scripture began to firmly take hold in my mind. In an effort for better understanding I began to read and reread the Bible, both, Old and New Testament alike, in various translations. This, I soon discovered, was an anomaly in modern Christianity. It seemed the emphasis was squarely on the New Testament, with little regard given to the very scriptures that Jesus and his followers quoted often. The popular stories of the Old Testament are, of course, used as examples of faith and to provide a moral foundation, but the vast majority of the Old Testament has either been ignored or written off as having been eclipsed by the New Testament. This is unfortunate because these are the very scriptures to which Jesus referred when preaching the good news of his Father's Kingdom. We know from the gospel of Luke that by the age of twelve Jesus was astounding the religious teachers in Jerusalem's temple, with his understanding of the scripture.[2] We also know from Matthew's gospel that Jesus quoted scripture to rebuff Satan's effort to tempt him into sinning.[3]

The Apostles also quoted extensively from Jewish scripture (the Old Testament in our Christian Bible). We have to remember that the original followers of Christ didn't consider themselves Christians in the modern sense. They considered themselves Jews; Jews who had witnessed the coming of their messiah as prophesied about in their scripture. For instance, Paul announced to the Jewish high council in Jerusalem, that he was a Pharisee, as were his ancestors.[4] He also wrote to Timothy about the usefulness of scripture:

> *You have been taught the Holy Scriptures from childhood, and they have given you the wisdom to receive the salvation that comes by trusting in Christ Jesus. All Scripture is inspired by God and is useful to teach us what is true and to make us realize what is wrong in our lives. It corrects us when we are wrong and teaches us to do what is right. God uses it*

to prepare and equip his people to do every good work. 2nd Timothy 3:15-17

So why would the very scriptures that were considered sacred by Jesus and his disciples, and which were integral to their ministry be less important today?

They aren't.

They're just as valuable; perhaps more so because Jesus came down to fulfill many of them by ushering in his Father's Kingdom. More importantly, when both testaments are used together, a clearer picture emerges as to the true intention of Christ and of the reasons why his life was sacrificed in the first place. As I read the Old Testament it became apparent that it doesn't allow for the idea of the Trinity at all with scriptures such as:

You have been chosen to know me, believe in me, and understand that I alone am God. There is no other God-there never has been, and there never will be. Isaiah 43:10

This is what the LORD says..."God is with you, and he is the only God. There is no other." Isaiah 45:14

I, the LORD your God, am a jealous God who will not tolerate your affection for any other gods. Exodus 20:5

and many more like them; there is very little chance that the god of the Old Testament shared his title as Supreme Being with anyone. It is made abundantly clear throughout the Old Testament as to who is in charge and what he wants: the LORD alone is God;[5] we should worship only the LORD as God;[6] the name of the LORD is to be remembered and respected.[7]

To put it in a different perspective I decided to simply count a few different phrases in the Bible to see if any patterns developed. The phrase *the LORD your God* occurs in the Old Testament nearly 400 times and the New Testament eight times. By contrast the phrase *Jesus your God* is never found in the Bible.

Never.

Moreover, the God of the Israelites used his own proper name often. For instance, he used the phrase *I am Yahweh* nearly 150 times in the Old Testament; out of the 150, he used the phrase *I am Yahweh your God* 36 times.[8] More importantly, Yahweh asks or, rather, demands to be worshiped in many scriptures. Jesus, on the other hand, never claimed to be God; he claimed to be the *Son of God.*[9] He also never asked to be worshiped. In fact, he's quite clear as to who should be, *"You must worship [Yahweh] the LORD your God and serve only him."*[10] Jesus also never claimed to be doing his will, but rather, the will of his Father who sent him.[11] Perhaps this is the reason the Old Testament isn't treated with the same type of authority as the New Testament; it doesn't help substantiate the belief in the Trinity. In fact, reading the Old Testament actually has the opposite effect on the manmade doctrine; it unravels it.

The third aspect of the Trinity, the *holy spirit* (also referred to as the *Holy Ghost*) is yet another concept that has no foundation in the Old Testament. Over the span of three centuries the substance of the *holy spirit* morphed from God's divine power or inspiration as it is actually portrayed in the Bible, into a third deity equal to both, God and Jesus. The actual phrase only appears in the Old Testament three times, none of which convey the idea that it's describing a deity. In fact, there isn't a single Old Testament scripture that even suggests that a second deity exists and comes down from heaven to either aide humans or dwell inside them.

The phrase *holy spirit* (along with others such as *divine spirit* or *spirit of holiness*) describes Yahweh's spirit, essence, or power: working through, inspiring, or being divinely bestowed upon and/or into a person. For instance, the prophets are spoken of as having been filled with God's *spirit of holiness*. And Yahweh spoke of *pouring* his spirit into the Israelites.[12] In fact, Peter recalled Joel 2:28 when describing a similar event that happened to him and other followers of Christ.[13] The gospel of John recorded that Jesus "*breathed*" on his disciples to impart his Father's spirit into them.[14] The spirit in these respects can best be likened to the energy current known in Chinese as qi (also known as chi), which is said to flow through us all and can be boosted through disciplined meditation.

Another apt example, albeit a fictional one, comes from George Lucas in his epic *Star Wars* saga. Lucas envisioned a universe wherein God is replaced by a power known as *the force.* This force, which binds together the universe and everything in it, has a good or light side, and an evil or dark side. As anyone who is familiar with the story knows either side could be embraced and, through disciplined study, mastered to gain supernatural power. The holy spirit emanating from God can be likened to the power which can be derived from *the force*.

While at times it is personified in the New Testament, the holy spirit is predominately referred to as either an abstraction or objectively. God's spirit is described in various scriptures as *filling up*, *falling upon*, or being *poured out* upon a person or persons. There are also several references of a person being baptized in it. The best example of this is found in Acts 10:38 when Peter declared that God anointed Jesus with his spirit. Here are all three facets of the so-called Godhead: Yahweh the Father, imparting his divine spirit, in the form of a dove, upon his son Jesus the messiah. Although this scripture has been said to reinforce the Trinity; the opposite, in fact, is the case. Jesus was *given* the power *by* his Father. This decries the concept of equality among the three as Yahweh has to be superior to both in order to be able to impart one (the spirit) to the other (Jesus); and Jesus must be below both, or he wouldn't have to have his Father impart the spirit upon him in the first place.

Interestingly enough, Jesus directly denied equality with the holy spirit. Three of the gospels record that Jesus emphatically declared the prominence of the holy spirit over himself: "*Anyone who speaks against the Son of Man can be forgiven, but anyone who speaks against the Holy Spirit will never be forgiven, either in this world or in the world to come.*" [15] Jesus clearly deferred to his Father's divine power, and stresses the dire consequences that come from denouncing it. This, however, seems to be overlooked entirely.

So how did Pastor Mark come to his conclusion on the existence of three separate but equal deities? Why would he and countless others teach an idea that is so obviously not scriptural, nor taught by Jesus and his early followers? I'm not sure about the others, but knowing

Mark, and knowing his heart, the only logical answer is that he is merely passing along what was taught to him to be true. This is understandable because we all tend to view the world through the lens with which we are given in childhood. What we're taught at an early age becomes ingrained into our psyche to the point of virtual immovability.

It's also inherent in humans to cling to the first version of anything as the "best," "correct" or "right" version. For instance, take a very simple, benign example of a movie remake. When Tim Burton announced he was going to remake *Willie Wonka and the Chocolate Factory*, a vast outcry grew from the generations that were raised on Gene Wilder's endearing portrayal of the eccentric candy purveyor. To these diehard fans remaking this timeless classic was bordering on sacrilege, but when the modern version was released a whole new generation was introduced to Johnny Depp's take on the Roald Dahl character, which understandably became their preeminent choice (I'm personally in the Wilder camp). The claims were also made that the modern movie is a visual masterpiece; a vast improvement over the old, outdated version (again, my vote is with the original).

This human trait is even more strongly prevalent when religion is involved. The specific religion or denomination (or the lack thereof) of our childhood becomes so enmeshed into our personalities that rarely can they become untangled without great difficulty. Christians that have switched denominations will always subconsciously point this out when the subject arises. Think about this, how many times have you heard someone say, "*Well, I was born Catholic, but...*"? I'm not picking on Catholics, I used them as my example because, well, *I* was born Catholic, but…

This example could just as well apply to any religion; simply replace Catholicism with the religion of your choice. The point is the religion of our childhood, and all of the manmade doctrine that comes with it, will always color our perceptions in some respect. It's very much like speaking a second language which was learned after childhood; it's virtually impossible not to talk with an accent. Likewise, when we are introduced to a different, perhaps controversial biblical teaching, we naturally filter it through our preconceived notions of what's correct based on our prior experiences and teachings from the first church to which we were exposed; but can we always trust what has been taught to us in church? Martin Luther didn't think so.

Christians should be seen and not heard

Martin Luther famously decried the Holy Roman Church's abusive practice of selling indulgences-salvation from eternal damnation for the living and for their deceased relatives, in return for money-starting a movement which would ultimately become known as the Protestant Reformation.

Originally, indulgences (absolution for sins, and from temporal punishment), could only be earned by Christians through confession and penance or, put another way, through prayer and specific good works. However, by the beginning of the 16th century, the original practice of granting indulgences by the Catholic Church had been subverted to include the ability to buy one's way out of trouble, and into heaven, along with the ability to buy indulgences for the souls of friends and relatives trapped in purgatory. This reached a zenith under Pope Leo X with his effort to construct St. Peter's Cathedral in Rome. Pope Leo X in 1517 commissioned Johann Tetzel, a Dominican monk, to head the collection of indulgences through all of Germany. He, and other monks from his order, combed the countryside selling salvation to any and all sinners, and for the souls of the damned.

Tetzel traveled from town to town, with an official letter from the Pope, which he read to the God-fearing masses. The letter guaranteed that the price of the indulgence was worth every groshen because not only were past sins of the purchaser forgiven, indeed, even sins not yet committed were covered under the papal blanket of absolution. Furthermore, for a not so small fee friends and relatives now suffering in purgatory could receive instantaneous release from their despair, to be delivered to heaven straightaway. This, of course, was all made possible because, as the letter stated, God no longer dealt with humans; God gave that power over to the Pope.

This isn't exactly what the Catholic Church intended when indulgences first became doctrine centuries earlier and Martin Luther knew it. So in a letter penned to his bishop, Albert of Mainz, on the 31st of October 1517 Luther voiced his opinions. This letter, which would become commonly known as *The Ninety-Five Theses*, listed all of the fallacies and distortions of canon that were being taught as doctrine. He challenged no less than the Pope himself when, in Theses 86, Luther compares the wealth of the Pope to Crassus (one of the wealthiest men of former Roman Empire). He contended that the Pope should build the St. Peter's Basilica with his own money, rather than with the money of poor believers. It was this and other writings by Luther, along his refusal to recant them under Papal order, which led to his excommunication from Roman Catholic Church.

The translating of *The Ninety-Five Theses* into German, from Latin, was the spark that would eventually light a fire in discontented churchgoers. This fire would engulf the Catholic Institution, leaving in its ashes a fractured church, with many former adherents turning to follow the teachings of Luther. This eventually grew into the Protestant Reformation that we know of today. Among his other notable achievements was his translating the Bible from its traditional language of Latin (the language of the clergy), into his people's native tongue of German. Luther believed that the lessons in the Bible were for all men. Consequently, he believed that the Bible should be accessible to the masses in their own language, eliminating the need for an outside interpreter. He felt in a large way the clergy was superfluous. He also believed that, under Christ, all are in the priesthood-not just the chosen few.

Great! Martin Luther reformed the church and became a hero to the people. Problem solved, right? Not so fast. While he made great strides advancing the message of Christ and making Bible available to the masses, Luther was still influenced by his earlier education, and by the opinions of many of his peers in faith. His anti-Semitism, for one thing, can be said to overshadow any good that the Reformation may have accomplished. In writings such as *On the Jews and Their Lies*, and *On the Holy Name and the Lineage of Christ*, both published in 1543, Luther pronounced Jews the devil's people, called for the seizing of their money and property, and for the destruction of their synagogues. Some scholars have said Luther's writings went so far as to have effectively called for their expulsions and deaths. This is obviously not the traditional portrait of the radical church reformer that is held up by his current admirers. There's more.

Luther also frowned on any scientific discoveries that went against traditional church teachings; writing against the findings of Copernicus in regard to the heliocentric system of the universe, believing it contradicted the Bible's teaching that the universe revolved around the earth. Luther pointed to scriptures such as, *"The sun rises and the sun sets, then hurries around to rise again,"*[16] *"You placed the world on its foundation so it would never be moved,"*[17] and to when Joshua prayed to Yahweh to *"let the sun and moon stand still"*[18] to discredit Copernicus. We now know, of course, that Copernicus was right all along. These scriptures were taken out of the context in which they were written; namely, that they would be read with the intention that they be understood from the perspective of the human viewer situated on earth. Interestingly enough, it seems it was the Protestant movement, and not the Roman Catholic Church, which proved to be the more intolerant. During Martin Luther's time the Catholic Church was ambivalent towards the ideas of Copernicus. Copernicus, who was educated in the Frombork Cathedral, even dedicated his controversial book *On the Revolutions of the Celestial Spheres*, to Pope Paul III.

Furthermore, Luther was a proponent of the witch-hunt craze that infected Germany and most of Europe, having been personally responsible for at least four burnings in Wittenberg, Germany. His opinion was that witches should be slain, since after all, they had made a pact with the devil. At least as many, if not more people were burned at the stake for witchcraft by Protestants than were killed for heresy by the Roman Church through their Inquisition. In retrospect, it seems that the Reformists weren't the most accepting bunch on the block. This brings us to yet another shining example of a church sanctioned practice which ultimately malformed into the wholesale practice of torturing and killing of suspected heretics.

The Roman Inquisition isn't the only instance of misguided zeal within the established Roman Catholic Church metastasizing into an abusive, power drunk monster. There were also the Medieval, Spanish and Portuguese Inquisitions; but, thanks to its treatment of Galileo and his writings, the Roman Inquisition is probably the most famous. The Inquisitions began with the Pope appointing cardinals to preside over tribunals that were originally created to stem the spread of the Protestant movement. They prosecuted individuals for a vast assortment of crimes, including blasphemy, heresy, sorcery and witchcraft. However, in their fury to stamp out the Reformation the tribunals began to increasingly rely on unsubstantiated rumors and outright torture during the vetting of suspected heretics. Many of the alleged heretics were put to death with only the slightest of reasons. This was sanctioned by the majority of church leaders up to and including the Popes; and all done in the name of God.

So much for religious tolerance.

Another aspect of their function was to censor any writings that were deemed too controversial or opposed the Church's teachings. To this end was committed much of the energy of the Roman Inquisition. Galileo Galilei, who has since been hailed as the father of modern science, was, during his lifetime, denounced by clerics to the Roman Inquisition in 1615. At that time he was cleared of wrongdoing, with the understanding that he agreed not to support the theory or talk further about it. Galileo, who could only hold his tongue for so long, eventually published *Dialogue concerning the Two Chief World Systems* in 1632. This book, which revived the subject of a universe that revolves around the sun, promptly led to his trial and conviction of heresy by the Inquisition. The same scriptures that Martin Luther used to "disprove" the findings of Copernicus were once again quoted, this time to validate the charges against Galileo.

The sentence imposed by the Roman Catholic Church forced Galileo to recant his support for Copernicus' heliocentric universe theory, forbade his publishing any further writings, and spend the rest of his life under house arrest. This was done with the knowledge and understanding by a large number of scientists and clerics that Galileo and Copernicus were right. Right or wrong, however, the Roman Catholic Church decided what was to be taught to the illiterate masses. This had been the norm since the middle of the 4th century, when Constantine unified the Roman Empire (combining paganism with Christianity in the process). In many ways the Catholic Church of today, with over a billion followers, still dramatically influences what's taught to one-sixth of the world's population.

A house divided will not stand

Finally, for those that believe *their* church couldn't possibly be teaching anything but accurate biblical doctrine, consider this: over a third of the world's population profess to be Christian. Simple enough, right? And I'm sure the biblical directive to *love our neighbors as ourselves* is a universal tenet. Nevertheless, man's ability to make even the most basic instruction more complex has brought us to our present dilemma of a fractured and ineffective Christian community. I suppose that's where we get the old expression: God is in the details. Or, is it: the devil is in the details?

I guess it depends on your attitude.

Nonetheless, there are presently over 9000 different Christian denominations represented in the *World Christian Database*, each one chock full of devout followers that believe their church understands the *true* meaning of Christianity.[19] This means that there were at least 9000 different occasions in the past, in which someone or some group felt strongly enough that they were being misled by their church as to cause their splintering off to start a new group. Most, if not all of these different groups believe in Christ and of the salvation he brings to those that accept it. Yet here we are, a fragmented silent majority bickering over petty doctrinal issues instead of trying to perpetuate a better society built upon the teachings of Christ. How did this happen?

While there have always been various splinter factions of Christianity competing with each other, the 11th century marked the first of the major splits within Orthodox Christianity. The Schism of 1054, which it has since been labeled, took place when Pope Leo IX excommunicated Michael Cerularius, the patriarch of the eastern branch of the State Church of the Roman Empire (later to become the Roman Catholic Church) located in Constantinople. This was done for a number of reasons, the least of which was Cerularius' refusal to accept the papal primacy of the Roman patriarch; Cerularius also ordered closed any Latin (western) church in Constantinople whose clergy refused to speak Greek instead of Latin from the pulpit. Not to be outdone Cerularius excommunicated the legates, the men who delivered the papal bull on behalf of the Pope.[20] The Greek branch, headquartered in Constantinople, would become the Eastern Orthodox Church.

The next major split would happen in England, when, in the 16th century Henry VIII, after unsuccessfully requesting an annulment from the Papacy, separated from the Roman Catholic Church, and made himself head of the newly formed Church of England. In addition to acquiring his annulment, Henry claimed for the Monarchy the huge fortunes that the various monasteries and churches had amassed and all the land they acquired in England over the years. The end of the 16th century brought Martin Luther's Reformation movement, which, coupled with the advent of the printing press, provided for the translation of the Holy Bible into the common languages of the lands-and into the hands of the people. This prompted a flurry of different denominations to spring up throughout Europe, England and eventually the New World.

Which brings us to today.

Taking into consideration the various languages that exist in the world, there are at last count, over 41,000 different Christian groups worldwide.[21] This is quite a large number of variations on such simple teachings as loving God and your neighbor. To put this figure into proper context, at this writing there are only 33,000 McDonald's restaurants worldwide. Many of these so-called Christian organizations are absolutely adamant that it's either their way or it's straight to hell. No if, ands or buts. They debate minutia without ever considering this small detail: would Jesus actually go through with what he did for all mankind just to keep people out on trivial technicalities such as whether or not to use leavened or unleavened bread during communion? It's highly doubtful. Yet denominations have been split over this very matter.

If Jesus came to replace the Mosaic Law, why are there still so many of them in Christendom? I don't remember him leaving a Torah-like textbook or list of statutes lying around for us to follow. Now before you get overly concerned, I'm not at all downplaying the New Testament's value. The New Testament gives us stories about the life of Jesus and his followers, and how future believers should try to live. However, it is unlike the Hebrew Torah (the first five books of the Old Testament) in which are found 613 different Mitzvoth, or commandments, involving all aspects of life.

Contrary to what is preached from the pulpit, there just aren't that many rules in the New Testament that one must follow in order to be a good Christian. There are just a few simple truths, some of which carry over from the Old Testament: worship only our heavenly Father and divine Creator with all our hearts, as he does us; his son Jesus is the messiah who came to fulfill all the old Jewish Covenant requirements; salvation comes with the acceptance of Jesus as the final sacrifice for all our sins once, and for all time; and, most importantly, that we should love our neighbors as ourselves. We are also given an idea of how Christian life should look if the above truths are believed and observed. That's it. And that's enough. After all, if we truly loved each other, what have we the need for laws?

This brings us back to my deserted island and Pastor Mark's belief in the Trinity. I became convinced that if he, or any of us for that matter, could clear our preconceived notions of what's written in the Bible and simply try to approach it with a fresh perspective, we would come to the conclusion that, contrary to popular opinion, there is a definite hierarchy within the Bible. First and foremost is Yahweh, the one and only true God, to whom we should all pray; second is Yahweh's divine spirit, which empowers all who ask of him for it; third is Yahweh's anointed son, Jesus, through which all sins are forgiven and through whom salvation from his Father is assured. Access to God and his divine spirit has been streamlined-thanks to Jesus.

Christians have, as a whole, forgotten the entire point of Christ, which was to bring us closer to God, not replace him. We have forgotten, pushed aside, or completely ignored Yahweh, the Supreme God, in favor of the Trinitarian doctrine of three equal gods constituting the Godhead. Worse yet, there is another doctrine that asserts that there has actually been only one being, who was first expressed as God in heaven, then as Jesus on earth, and finally as the holy spirit. This theory, called Oneness, is even more convoluted (and unscriptural) then the Trinity.

Far too often scriptures that don't jibe with the concept of the Trinity (or Oneness) are casually brushed aside, such as when Jesus appeared to Mary Magdalene after his resurrection, and told her to *"go find my brothers and tell them that I am ascending to my Father and your Father, to my God and your God,"*[22] or when Jesus told his disciples that he was *"going to the Father, who is greater than I am."*[23]

We have been taught to ignore God's simple requests to remember his name, to worship him alone, and to believe and appreciate that Jesus was sacrificed so that we all could draw closer to his Father. We have been taught to ignore that Jesus spoke only of his Father's will and of his Father's heavenly Kingdom; that his power came from his Father; and that he is, in all manners subordinate to both his Father, and to his Father's spirit. We have been taught to ignore that Jesus was very clear as to whom it is we are to worship, constantly pointing to scripture to show his followers. Alone and without outside intervention, we would understand that the Bible is quite clear as to the importance of whom we should be praying. We would discover that Yahweh is the lost god of Christianity; the lost god of Christ.

The Bible is clear on these basic tenets. If it is ambiguous on a subject that subject probably isn't that crucial. That's why a person reading the Bible for the first time on a deserted island wouldn't have a problem discerning the essential teachings. Unfortunately, we can't unlearn what we have been taught; we can't undo our past. We can, however, question our beliefs grounded in the past and inform ourselves for the future. This book is intended to help do just this. It's meant to help guide the reader through the biases that have accumulated through the years, and sift through the unbiblical doctrine that pervades mainstream Christianity, starting with the name of God.

2 What's in a name?

> *The LORD says, "I was ready to respond, but no one asked for help. I was ready to be found, but no one was looking for me. I said, 'Here I am, here I am!' to a nation that did not call on my name.* Isaiah 65:1

Did you ever notice that Christian songs are constantly singing about the name of God, and praising the name of God, but very seldom does the song actually say the name of God? I did. An excellent example of this is "Blessed be the name of the Lord" by Matt Redman. Although it's a beautiful song it never actually mentions God's name.[24]

I also noticed that Christians virtually never say God's name when praying aloud. And no, *The Big Man Upstairs* doesn't count. If you haven't noticed then you're probably like the many other Christians who aren't even aware that God has a name. By the way, *God* isn't a name, and neither is *Lord* or *Father*. These are generic titles that can be used to describe other deities and even humans. And contrary to the teachings of certain Christian denominations his proper name isn't Jesus. Jesus is the *son of God*, as is evidenced by numerous scriptures.

So does God even have a personal name as we understand the concept of names? More importantly, if he has a proper name does it matter whether or not that we use it?

Absolutely it does. Scripture is very clear on this.

For instance, Peter pointed this out to a crowd of onlookers in Jerusalem when he said that "*everyone who calls on the name of the LORD will be saved."*[25] Time after time the Bible also consistently shows the importance of worshiping the only true God, both, in the Old and New Testament. It is, in fact, the first of the Ten Commandments, "*I am the LORD your God...You must not have any other god but me.*"[26] The idea of one true god, with that God being referred to as "*the LORD,*" is supported throughout scripture:

> *Listen, O Israel! The LORD is our God, the LORD alone. And you must love the LORD your God with all your heart, all your soul, and all your strength.* Deuteronomy 6:4-5

> *"You have been chosen to know me, believe in me, and understand that I alone am God. There is no other God— there never has been, and there never will be... You are witnesses that I am the only God," says the LORD. "From eternity to eternity I am God."* Isaiah 43:10, 12-13

> *You must worship the LORD your God and serve only him.* Matthew 4:10

Without knowing the name of God how can we truly call on him? This is suggested by the scripture from Isaiah that opened this section, and by the words of Peter. After all, we can't call on the name of *the LORD* if we don't know that name.

The NLT Bible (from which I quote extensively throughout this book), as well as other translations, spells out lord in all capital letters (LORD) in these and thousands of other scriptures. What if anything does this denote? In addition, since both testaments use the term lord quite frequently to denote Jesus as well as God, is this significant? Is Jesus Christ the Lord of the Old Testament? To answer these questions we need to do a little research into the origins of the different English names applied to God in the Bible. Before we do that, though, a small history lesson about monotheism is in order. For those of us that fell asleep in history class I'll try to make this as painless as possible. This is what's referred to as a necessary evil.

Blessed be the name of the LORD?

> *Blessed be the name of the LORD now and forever.* Psalm 113:2

The origins of Christianity can be traced back to a place and time when all Christians were Jewish. These Jewish followers of Yashua ha Mashiach, better known as Jesus the messiah, believed he was their anointed savior as foretold in their Jewish scripture. Jesus and his followers practiced Judaism, an ancient religion that was unlike its contemporary counterparts; Judaism is monotheistic, meaning it espoused the necessity of worshipping the single, supreme God, as described in their scripture. Other religions of that era weren't so particular; one could worship any number of gods, none of whom would be offended for having to share the spotlight with their godly peers. However, the Jewish God was different; he commanded absolute sovereignty. Although the concept of monotheism might have shown up briefly in other cultures, it was with the Israelites that the idea firmly took hold.

We learn from Jewish scripture (the Old Testament in Christian Bibles) the history of the Israelites and of their relationship with their supreme God. Their national story begins in the twelfth chapter of Genesis with *"the LORD"* sending Abram (soon to be renamed Abraham) on a journey, telling Abram that he would be blessed, and become a great nation. Here is the beginning of monotheism as embraced by Abraham and continued with his descendants.

It should be pointed out, that although the majority of the Israelites were descendants of Abraham, this wasn't a requirement. *"The LORD"* said to Abram that all the clans of the earth will be blessed through him.[27] Right from the start there have been examples in the Bible of foreigners who turned away from their beliefs to follow the customs of the Israelites. In fact, there is mention of outsiders joining the Israelites in the exclusive worship of their God throughout the Old Testament. Many scriptures highlight this confluence of followers.

For instance, the Israelites are described in Joshua as *"foreign and native born alike."*[28] Also, during the dedication ceremony of the newly built temple, Solomon proclaimed that people from distant lands would come to pray at the temple where "*the LORD*" would hear them and grant their requests. "*The LORD*" actually handed down directions on how these converts were to be accepted into the faith by the Israelites:

> *Do not take advantage of foreigners who live among you in your land. Treat them like native-born Israelites, and love them as*

> *you love yourself. Remember that you were once foreigners living in the land of Egypt. I am the LORD your God.* Leviticus 19:33-34

> *Native-born Israelites and foreigners are equal before the LORD and are subject to the same decrees.* Numbers 15:15

During this early time in their history, the Israelites lived continually among other cultures, most of which worshipped a pantheon of other pagan gods. The older books of the Hebrew Bible often referred to these gods. In fact, some of the very names used for the God of the Israelites in the Old Testament were probably borrowed from these other cultures. El, El Elyon, and El Shaddai, for instance, are all believed to be archaic names of Canaanite gods, which have since been absorbed and reused by the Israelites when referring to their own God. (Citizens of the United States have co-opted the term *America* as another name for our country in much the same way.) It should be noted that throughout the Old Testament one of the main failings of the Israelites was their constant turning away from their "*LORD*" to worship these other gods, which helps to explain why the names were absorbed in the first place.

Now, let's jump to the book of Exodus, where "*the LORD*" spoke to Moses from the burning bush about the plight of his people, the Israelites, and Moses' upcoming task of leading them out of Egypt. After "*the LORD*" described himself as the God of Moses' ancestors (Abraham, Isaac and Jacob) Moses asked "*the LORD:*"

> *Look, when I come to the Israelites and say to them, "The God of your fathers has sent me to you," and they say to me, "What is His name?" what shall I say to them?* Exodus 3:13[29]

God responded with three answers to the question. The first two are somewhat cryptic, but the third answer gives us the true, proper name of God. Here are the first two:

> *And God said to Moses, "'Ehyeh-'Asher-'Ehyeh, I Will-Be-Who-I-Will-Be." And He said, "Thus shall you say to the Israelites, ' Ehyeh has sent me to you.'"* Exodus 3:14[30]

The meaning of the phrase *'Ehyeh-'Asher-'Ehyeh,* as it has traveled through the millennia, has become unclear. While many Bible versions tend to translate *'Ehyeh* as *I am* this is almost certainly incorrect. The more probable translation is *I will be* or *I shall be,* which is how it is used in many other scriptures.[31] Professor Robert Alter, the preeminent scholar on biblical Hebrew and Hebrew literature, gives us insight as to the different possible translations of the phrase, "'I-Will-Be-Who-I-Will-Be' is the most plausible construction of the Hebrew, though the middle word, 'asher, could easily mean 'what' rather than 'who'…'"[32]

Furthermore, Professor Alter adds that because of the differences between the tense systems of biblical Hebrew and English in regard to sentence structure, it's possible for the phrase to mean, "*I am he who endures.*" To put it simply, although "*I will be who I will be*" is probably the most accurate translation, no one really knows unequivocally. The next sentence, "*Ehyeh has sent me to you*" translates to "*I will be has sent me to you.*" While this is a slightly more straightforward answer it's still more of a declaration than proper name. Moses had twice protested God's decision and, thus, God's impatience with Moses can be sensed in these first two responses. However, in verse fifteen God reveals his own divine name:

> *And God said further to Moses, "Thus shall you say to the Israelites: The LORD God of your fathers, the God of Abraham, the God of Isaac, and the God of Jacob, sent me to you.*
>
> *That is My name forever*
> *And thus am invoked in all ages."*[33]

Thus we have the proper name of God given to us by God.

The LORD God.

Only, what exactly does God mean in this sentence? Is the personal name of the God of the Israelites *the LORD*, *God*, or *the LORD God*? And why is lord in all capital letters? Does it signify anything? Finally, do these words carry the same meaning throughout the entire Bible? To answer these questions we need to have a quick lesson in biblical Hebrew.

I know, I know.

Learning a bit of Hebrew probably wasn't what you had in mind when you picked up this book but it's important if we want to get to the bottom of this *the LORD God* puzzle. Just hang in there.

The most common reference to the god of the Israelites is known today by scholars as the Tetragrammaton. The term Tetragrammaton is derived from Greek meaning *four letter word.* The four letters represented by the Hebrew characters - י - ה - ו - ה - are pronounced *yod-heh-vav-heh.* They are known by their English letter equivalents of Y-H-W-H.[34] This four letter word, pronounced *yah-weh*, is found 6828 times in the Old Testament alone. Yahweh is the proper name of God as given to Moses by God himself. And while many of his attributes have been listed as names for God by overzealous Christians, Yahweh is the only proper name given to him in the Bible. His attributes only seem to be other names because the Hebrew words are used instead of their English equivalents. For instance, *Yahweh-Yireh*, *Yahweh-Sabaoth* and *Yahweh-Raah* simply mean *Yahweh will provide*, *Yahweh of hosts* and *Yahweh is my shepherd* respectively.[35]

The god of the Hebrews has only one true name, Yahweh. Here is another example of a word that has, down through the ages, almost been forgotten. This time, however, it's not the definition, but its importance which has been lost.

The main catalyst for this was a practice that began centuries before the birth of Christ. Sometime in the history of the Hebrews a prohibition on pronouncing the name Yahweh started to be observed by many Israelites; this stemmed from the fear of accidentally misusing the divine name. Eventually only the High Priest was said to have used the otherwise ineffable name, and only on the Day of Atonement, and only in the center of the temple compound known as the Holy of Holies. The detrimental ban on pronouncing God's name stemmed from yet another example of taking scripture entirely out of context.

In many places the Bible insists upon the veneration of the sacred name of Yahweh, with harsh stipulations against the misuse or slander of it found throughout. After all, one of the Ten Commandments is not to take Yahweh's name in vain. This healthy reverence adhered to by the Jews somehow devolved over the centuries to the near total abandonment of using his name. So resolved was their misguided zeal to protect the sanctity of his name, stories abound of their inability to destroy texts that spoke against Yahweh simply because they feared the written name was in itself sacred. In their minds, even though these texts may have defamed Yahweh, destroying the paper upon which the name was written became the bigger transgression. Consequently, to this day many Jews will either write a stand-in for the name or intentionally misspell it; some have even taken it to the extreme case of spelling God without the O, as in G_D. In addition, when reading scripture aloud rather than saying the name of God, whenever they come to it the word is revocalized to *ha Shem*; *Ha Shem* simply means *the name* in Hebrew. This is not at all what Yahweh had in mind as is evident by the dozens of times that the Bible demands that his name be remembered and worshipped. The name Yahweh is found in the Bible nearly 7000 times for a reason!

Eventually, its pronouncement was forgotten or ignored by all but the priestly class. With the destruction of the Jewish temple by the Babylonians in 586 B.C.E., the priests, for a time, lost virtually all of their importance. The name Yahweh was, accordingly, nearly lost through disuse.[36] We have to keep in mind that the original Hebrew texts were written in consonants only. Vowels were added at a much later date; long after the prohibition on vocalizing the name was established. So although we have the consonants Y-H-W-H, the vowels are an educated guess. Most biblical scholars generally agree on its present pronouncement for a few reasons. First, scholars refer to Greek transcriptions of Hebrew texts to give insight to its pronunciation. Additionally, Yah is another name used in Hebrew texts for the Jewish God. For instance, Isaiah 12:2 reads: "*For YAH, the LORD, is my strength and song; He also has become my salvation*" (NKJV).

Yah is just a shortened form of Yahweh.[37]

These reasons strongly suggest Yahweh as the proper pronouncement. The use of yah as a suffix in words such as hallelujah, which means *praise Yahweh* and names such as Uriah and Jedidiah, which mean *Yahweh is my light* and *friend of Yahweh* respectively, also lends support to this conclusion. (We will discover why hallelujah is spelled with a j and not a y in a little later.)

What does this have to do with "*the LORD God*" of the Bible, you ask?

Just this: by the time Jewish scripture was translated into Greek, the name YHWH had undergone a transformation. Its original Hebrew pronunciation of *Yahweh* had been revocalized by Jews to the Hebrew word *adonai*, which means *lord*, or *master*. Subsequently, even though the name should have been pronounced *Yahweh* it was instead pronounced *adonai*, causing much confusion during the scripture's translation into Greek, and then later, into other languages. The result is that God's proper name, Yahweh, has been mistakenly replaced in most Bibles by the phrase *the Lord.* The translation that started this practice, *The King James Bible,* acknowledges this (as do other translations) by writing lord in all capitals, i.e. LORD. So wherever the words *the LORD* appear, they're replacing *Yahweh*, the proper Hebrew name of the God of the Israelites.

Don't believe me?

Check the introduction of your Bible.

There is something else we should also remember; the name Yahweh is never used to designate anyone other than the Almighty God of the Israelites. This is his proper name and no one else's. Yahweh is the name professed by God himself; a name he directly recited to Moses. The following scriptures reinforce this:

> *You alone are* ***[Yahweh]*** *the LORD.* Nehemiah 9:6

> *Then they will learn that you alone are called* ***[Yahweh]*** *the LORD, that you alone are the Most High, supreme over all the earth.* Psalm 83:18

> *It is I,* ***[Yahweh]*** *the LORD, the First and the Last. I alone am he.* Isaiah 41:4

> *I, yes I, am* ***[Yahweh]*** *the LORD, and there is no other Savior.* Isaiah 43:11

> *They will know that I alone am* ***[Yahweh]*** *the LORD.* Ezekiel 6:10

The transposing of *the LORD* for *Yahweh* causes confusion and makes scripture difficult to follow for a few reasons. First, few people are aware that the substitution is even happening. Consequently, the assumption can easily be made that the phrase *the Lord Jesus* in the New Testament is *the LORD* of the Old Testament. It's a fairly easy assumption to make under the circumstance, but, as we'll see, a potentially disastrous one. Second, there are Hebrew texts with the words *Yahweh* and *adonai* in the same sentence. An excellent example of this is Psalm 110:1. Traditionally, the scripture ambiguously reads, "*The LORD said to my Lord, "Sit in the place of honor at my right hand until I humble your enemies, making them a footstool under your feet."* However, if accurately translated the scripture would read, *"[Yahweh's] utterance to my master: "Sit at My right hand till I make your enemies a stool for your feet."*[38] Considering that Jesus quoted this scripture,[39] as did the Apostle Peter,[40] the importance of accuracy is even greater.

There is a final problem regarding the use of the word lord in the New Testament. It is the subtle but misleading manner in which the word is capitalized. In many translations only the first letter is capitalized when referring to Christ (Lord); while all of the letters are capitalized when the text is quoting an Old Testament scripture that contains the name Yahweh (LORD); in all other circumstances it is printed entirely in lowercase letters (lord). Translating the word in this manner gives the false impression that Yahweh is only found in the New Testament within the context of Jewish scripture. In other words it presupposes that the men of the New Testament only referred to Yahweh in the context of Old

Testament quotes. Thus all other uses, by default, must refer to Jesus. This is a very deceptive because the men of the New Testament, including Jesus himself, constantly referred to Yahweh outside of the context of Jewish scripture.

For instance, Peter preached to a crowd that "*the Lord our God*" will pour out his spirit into everyone, Jews and Gentiles alike.[41] We can see from the context of the entire chapter that Peter's use of the title God is in direct reference to Yahweh *(the LORD)*; his quoting Joel 2:28-32 and Psalm 16:8-11 makes this abundantly clear. We also notice that Peter always clearly differentiated between God and Jesus. Consequently, when Peter said "*the Lord our God*" the correct translation would be *Yahweh our God*, or, at the very least, *the LORD our God.*

The same can be said about the use of "*the Lord*" when Paul proclaimed that, "*the Lord gave us this command,*"[42] then referenced Isaiah 49:6; when James talked of "*the prophets who spoke in the name of the Lord;*"[43] and when Peter showed through the stories of Noah and Sodom and Gomorrah that, "*the Lord knows how to rescue godly people from their trials.*"[44] Elizabeth, an elderly Jewish woman exclaimed, *"How kind the Lord is!"*[45] after she discovered that she became pregnant at an advanced age. As a devout Jew she would only be thanking her God for her soon to be born son. It also apparent that when Luke mentioned the "*God of the Israelites,*" or to the *"sanctuary of the Lord"* he is referring to Yahweh. [46]

In all of the above instances it is obvious that "*the Lord*" refers to none other than Yahweh, the God of the Israelites, and should be written in such a manner as to relay this. We have to keep in mind that the oldest surviving Greek manuscripts were written in all capital letters so modern translators are making their own decisions as to capitalizations; they're not simply transcribing the texts letter for letter, or even word for word for that matter; they're making decisions affected in no small part by their biases.

There are other scriptures in which *the Lord* and Jesus are mentioned together, such as when the angel Gabriel visited Mary to tell her that she would have a baby who will be named Jesus, will be called son of the Most High, and will be given the throne of David by "*the Lord God.*" [47] We can ascertain that *the Lord God* refers to none other than Yahweh himself. Zechariah also gave a prophecy about Jesus, which begins, *"Praise the Lord, the God of Israel... He has sent us a mighty Savior."*[48] Once again there can be no question that Zechariah was referring to Yahweh, "*the God of Israel,*" when he said "*praise the Lord.*" Shortly after Christ's ascension, Peter addressed a crowd in the Jerusalem temple telling them that God would once again send Jesus, their messiah to right the world; Peter quoted Deuteronomy 18:15 to qualify his statement, *"[Yahweh] the LORD your God will raise up for you a Prophet like me from among your own people."*[49] Finally, it is revealed in a vision to John of Patmos that the new temple of Jerusalem would be "*the Lord God Almighty and the Lamb.*"[50]

There are many other New Testament scriptures that use *the lord* together with Old Testament references, as when prophecies of are pronounced fulfilled; two of such refer to the messiah being called out of Egypt, and to his healing the sick as foretold in Hosea ll:1 and Isaiah

53:4 respectively.[51] By mentioning both the Lord and Jesus (or some reference to Jesus) in the above scriptures there is no doubt that *the Lord* is referring Yahweh.

Then, of course, there are the scriptures in which Jesus is clearly talking about his God. As an example, he told his disciples to "*pray to the Lord who is in charge of the harvest; ask him to send more workers into his fields.*"[52] Jesus also said that Moses referred to the Lord, as "*the God of Abraham, the God of Isaac and the God of Jacob.*"[53] In both instances Jesus could have only been referring to Yahweh.

Now let's take a look at some popular Jewish phrases that bridge both testaments. There are several phrases used in the New Testament that followers of Judaism would have immediately recognized from their Bible as referring to Yahweh: *Angel of the Lord*,[54] *Spirit of the Lord*,[55] *the Lord of Heaven's Armies*,[56] and *the Lord God*.[57] Taken in their proper context all of these phrases are undeniably referring to Yahweh. Finally, we have the phrase *Hallelujah* found in Revelation 19:1, 3, 4, and 6. Hallelujah, as we've learned, actually means *praise Yah* a contracted form of Yahweh.

Surreptitiously removing the name of God from the Bible causes quite a few problems. First and foremost, without knowing about the substitution of *the LORD* for *Yahweh* the assumption that *"the Lord Jesus"* and "*the LORD God*" of the Old Testament are the same being seems plausible; second, New Testament scriptures referring to Yahweh are mistakenly attributed to Jesus because of the way the word *lord* is handled. Thus the line between the Jesus and God gets sufficiently blurred as to cause confusion.

However, with a little insight we can see that, in reality, the word *lord* has many uses; we can see that the original texts of the Bible very clearly drew a distinction between Jesus and Yahweh. This distinction has been removed from modern Bibles. The more accurate way to render the texts has been continually ignored for the sake of tradition, and, as we'll see, to further manmade doctrine. Unfortunately, there doesn't seem to be any signs of this changing. (We will soon see that similar problems surround the use of the word god.)

Are you still with me? Mazel tov! We're almost done with the Hebrew portion of today's lesson. Then we can dive into scripture to understand their true meaning and intention.

In God we Trust

> *There may be so-called gods both in heaven and on earth, and some people actually worship many gods and many lords. But we know that there is only one God, the Father, who created everything, and we live for him. And there is only one Lord, Jesus Christ, through whom God made everything and through whom we have been given life.*
>
> 1st Corinthians 8:5-6

Now, what about the word *god*? We find it being used in a large variety of situations throughout the Bible. The question is why? Isn't it just another name, like Yahweh? Doesn't it mean the same thing in every instance? For instance, the prophet Isaiah referred to Jesus as *mighty*

God.[58] Does calling Jesus mighty god equate him with Yahweh? It depends on the meaning of the word *god.*

The Hebrew word translated as god in English is *'elohim*, which is the second most used designation (after Yahweh) for the God of Israel in the Old Testament; however, *'elohim* has numerous other uses in the Bible.[59] *'Elohim* is also used to refer to divine messengers, subordinate gods (e.g. where Yahweh is compared to pagan gods, or when Yahweh is speaking about other heavenly beings, including his son), spirits and men. The same goes for *theos*, the Greek word for god used in the New Testament. In fact, Paul even used it to describe the devil in a letter to Corinth.

Yes, the word *god* is also used to describe Satan.

First, let's start with Abraham. He was talking to a pagan, Abimelech, when he said, "*And it happened, when the gods made me a wanderer from my father's house...*"[60] In this instance, *'elohim* is used by Abraham in its plural form to make a reference that covers both his belief in Yahweh, and Abimelech's belief in pagan gods. Further down the word *'elohim* is used by the Hittites referring to Abraham. Properly translated the scripture would read, "*Pray, hear us, my lord. You are a prince of gods among us!*"[61] Considering the Hittites were pagan and had multiple gods there wasn't any chance they were referring exclusively to Yahweh. Consequently, here the word *'elohim* should probably be translated as a *preeminent dignitary*; nonetheless, it shows the diversity of the word's usage.

In another example Yahweh spoke to Moses, saying that he would be godlike over his brother Aaron.[62] Further along Yahweh prepared Moses for his meeting with Pharaoh by telling him, "*See, I have set you as a god to Pharaoh, and Aaron your brother will be your prophet.*"[63] In both of these instances the word used to describe Moses was *'elohim.* Yahweh then announces to the Israelites (through Moses and Aaron) that he would "*execute judgment against all the gods of Egypt, for I am [Yahweh] the LORD!*"[64] As we can read in the book of Numbers, Yahweh was true to his word, "*The LORD [Yahweh] had defeated the gods of Egypt that night with great acts of judgment!*"[65] Once again, it is the same Hebrew word *'elohim* that has been translated to *gods.*

In yet another use of the word *'elohim* we find that during a séance Samuel's spirit was described by the medium as a god rising up from earth.[66] Further, the Psalmist wrote that Yahweh judged *heavenly beings*, a *divine council*, or *gods*, depending on the translation; earthly leaders were also referred to as gods in this Psalm.[67] We can see that the same Hebrew word, '*elohim*, is used throughout to describe God, those that God judged, and the earthly rulers. In fact, Jesus quoted this very scripture while defending himself to a violent crowd: "*It is written in your own Scriptures that God said to certain leaders of the people, 'I say, you are gods!*'"[68] Finally, Paul referred to Satan as *ho theos tou aionos*, or *the god of this age.*[69]

One thing is very clear, the use of the word god does not automatically refer to Yahweh, the Israelite God of Abraham, Isaac, and Jacob; nor does it replace Yahweh as the personal and proper name of God. In fact, many scriptures combine both words to ensure there is no mistaking as to whom the scripture is referring, including Exodus 3:15:

> *God ['elohim] also said to Moses, "Say this to the people of Israel: Yahweh, the God ['elohim] of your ancestors—the God ['elohim] of Abraham, the God ['elohim] of Isaac, and the God ['elohim] of Jacob—has sent me to you.*
>
> *This is my eternal name,*
> *My name to remember for all generations."*

Here we have it. Yahweh spelled it out for Moses (and for everyone else). Yahweh is his name, and we are all to remember it. Scripture, properly restored with the true name of God, reinforce the requirement for us to acknowledge his name:

> *I am [**Yahweh**]... your God...you must not have any other god but me.* Exodus 20:2-3
>
> *Listen, O Israel! [**Yahweh**]... is our God, [**Yahweh**]... alone. And you must love [**Yahweh**]... your God with all your heart, all your soul, and all your strength.* Deuteronomy 6:4-5
>
> *You must worship no other gods, for [**Yahweh**]... whose very name is Jealous, is a God who is jealous about his relationship with you.* Exodus 34:14
>
> *Serve [**Yahweh**]... alone.* Joshua 24:14

*For [**Yahweh**]... your God is the supreme God of the heavens above and the earth below.* Joshua 2:11

*Jesus [said], "The most important commandment is this: 'Listen, O Israel! [**Yahweh**]... our God is the one and only [**Yahweh**]. And you must love [**Yahweh**]... your God with all your heart, all your soul, all your mind, and all your strength.'"*
Mark 12:29-30

*Jesus [said], "The Scriptures say, 'You must worship [**Yahweh**]... your God and serve only him.'"* Luke 4:8

The name of God has been properly reinstated in the above scriptures to reveal their original, true meaning. That's just seven examples. Imagine if the name was restored to the other nearly 7000 places it was improperly removed? The name would take on an entirely new significance; a significance that should have never been lost in the first place. Both the name and the deity of Yahweh would take on an entirely new importance to Christians. Finally, just in case there was any uncertainty left, Yahweh tried to ensure that Moses and future generations would make no mistake in regard to him and his name:

And God said to Moses, "I am Yahweh— 'the LORD.' I appeared to Abraham, to Isaac, and to Jacob as El-Shaddai—'God

Almighty'—but I did not reveal my name, Yahweh, to them. Exodus 6:2-3

Does not a rose by any other name…

Not everyone who calls out to me, 'Lord! Lord!' will enter the Kingdom of Heaven. Only those who actually do the will of my Father in heaven will enter. Matthew 7:21

At this point you might be saying to yourself, "Well how much does it really matter? After all, God gets the idea. He knows that we love him, right?" That depends on whether or not we're giving him the proper respect due to him as the divine creator of the universe. We have to be careful that our intent isn't misguided. The blurring of lines between Yahweh and Jesus has led to some conclusions that might not be biblical. Let's see what the scriptures have to say about the importance of Yahweh's name.

Let's begin with the number of times it was used in the Bible. As I mentioned earlier, the name Yahweh was originally found 6828 times in the Old Testament alone. From a purely mathematical point of view any name that's used nearly 7000 times has to be fairly important. To contrast, the name Jesus (referring to the messiah) is found less than a 1000 times in the New Testament.[70]

The use of Yahweh in the New Testament is a source of heated debate among scholars. The old consensus is that it wasn't used much, if at all, by early Christian writers. However, as the discovery of ancient manuscripts shed new light on the subject, some scholars are rethinking this belief. One thing we can be sure about is that Jesus and his disciples consistently quoted scripture from their Jewish texts, many of which contained the name Yahweh. Whether the writers of the letters and texts of what eventually would become the New Testament actually wrote down the name Yahweh, or some substitute, everyone knew to whom they were referring.

A great example is during the temptation of Christ in the wilderness by Satan, in which Jesus quoted from Deuteronomy three times.[71] All three scriptures contained his Father's name, Yahweh. The first was in response to Satan telling Jesus to turn stones into bread to satisfy his hunger (Jesus had been fasting there for forty days):

> *People do not live by bread alone; rather, we live by every word that comes from the mouth of [Yahweh]...* Deuteronomy 8:3

Then, Satan brought Jesus to the top of the temple in Jerusalem and, also quoting scripture, told Jesus to jump off:

> *If you are the Son of God, jump off! For the Scriptures say, "He will order his angels to protect you. And they will hold you up with their hands so you won't even hurt your foot on a stone."* Psalm 91:11-12

Incidentally, it is interesting that Satan used scripture in an attempt to challenge God's power and Jesus' authority. This shows Satan's ability to use the very things that are held most dear to those whom he tempts.

How did Jesus respond? With yet another scripture showing God's authority:

> *You must not test [Yahweh]... your God.*
> Deuteronomy 6:16

Finally, Satan told Jesus he would give him all the kingdoms of the world if he would just bow and worship him. Jesus responded directly and to the point:

> *"Get out of here, Satan," Jesus told him. "For the Scriptures say, 'you must worship [Yahweh]... your God and serve only him.'"* Deuteronomy 6:13

Considering that Jesus was Jewish, as were most if not all of his early disciples, there is no doubt they would consider scriptures sacred. Neither Jesus nor his disciples would intentionally misquote them, nor would they deny the importance of the name Yahweh. Yet this is exactly what many translations have done.

Let's pause here for a moment to point out a very real problem with Bible translations that have taken too many liberties with their interpretation. There is a very real possibility that, when trying to change a subject matter in an effort to make it easier to understand, the true message will get, blurred, tainted or possibly lost entirely. This is true in any field of interest or profession. Most subjects are replete with books, magazines, trade journals and textbooks written with various degrees of detail and information for a reason. For instance, a casual car enthusiast might be satisfied with a publication that gives a general description of a vehicle's engine, transmission and chassis, but a mechanic would be unable to perform even the most remedial repairs without a detailed manual. For these individuals trade journals and textbooks are essential. So as the desire or need increases for more detailed information, the demand for accuracy is also increased dramatically. This demand for accuracy holds true for the Bible more than for any other subject. If this weren't the case we could all trade in our eleven hundred-page Bible for a children's edition, chock full of pictures, and without all those tedious genealogy lists. Imagine the satisfaction we would get in being able to read the entire Bible every day!

The truth of the matter is that children's Bibles serve a very valuable purpose. They introduce our children to the myriad of characters and stories in the Bible without overwhelming them with too much information. Using very broad strokes, a child's Bible paints a beautiful portrait of all the wondrous occurrences therein, without it being muddied by less important details-such as all the tedious genealogy lists. (I know the entire Bible is important, but why don't you try reading the 26th chapter of Numbers to your five year old and then get back to me.) As we grow and advance in our understanding, however, the need increases for a more detailed translation of the Bible, with scriptural accuracy, so we are better able to understand the deeper nuances and subtleties found within its pages. Eventually, we even come to appreciate those very tedious genealogy lists, which, incidentally, are the threads that bind together the two testaments and give us some insight to historical timelines.

Unfortunately, in using common parlance some modern Bibles have compromised accuracy for ease in understanding. One recent translation, *The Message Bible*, has completely removed both the name Yahweh, and its alternate designation, the LORD, choosing instead to use the word god throughout. This is exactly what Yahweh didn't want. In scripture after scripture he demanded his name be remembered, but in this translation it has actually been erased entirely. Here are just a few of the many scriptures that reinforce the importance of remembering his name:

> *I am [Yahweh]... that is my name! I will not give my glory to anyone else, nor share my praise with carved idols.* Isaiah 42:8

> *[Yahweh]... says, "I will rescue those who love me. I will protect those who trust in my name.* Psalm 91:14

> *I will reveal my name to my people, and they will come to know its power.* Isaiah 52:6

> *When you swear by my name, saying, "As surely as [Yahweh]... lives," you could do so with truth, justice, and righteousness. Then you would be a blessing to the nations of the world, and all people would come and praise my name.* Jeremiah 4:2

> *Jesus said, "This is how you should pray: Father, may your name be kept holy."*
> Luke 11:2

> *I [Yahweh] held back in order to protect the honor of my name...* Ezekiel 20:14

> *They will call on my name, and I will answer them. I will say, "These are my people," and they will say, "[Yahweh]... is our God."*
> Zechariah 13:9

The above list of scriptures is by no means inclusive. Pick up your Bible and see for yourself. You'll be surprised at how many times *the LORD* will jump off the page, now that you are aware of its substitution for God's actual name. You will soon understand its significance, not only to God, but to his prophets, to his son and, hopefully, to you.

3 Jesus

> *I am the light of the world. If you follow me, you won't have to walk in darkness, because you will have the light that leads to life.*
>
> John 8:12

Now that we know that Yahweh is the personal name of God and the different meanings of *LORD*, *Lord* and *God*, it's time to see where Jesus Christ fits into all of this. Is he *the* God found in the Old Testament? To put it another way, are Jesus Christ and Yahweh one and the same, as some denominations teach? Or are they, as others believe, different but equal? These concepts are the fundamental bases of the Oneness and Trinity doctrines, which suppose that Jesus, Yahweh, and the holy spirit are either the same, single God in different form, or that they are different but equal parts of a singular deity.

By far, these are the most popular concepts taught in Christian churches around the world; but are they accurate? As we discovered in the past chapter it's safe to say that, at least in the Old Testament, Yahweh reigns supreme. He and all his prophets were very adamant about this. The Old Testament very clearly laid the foundation of monotheism; the worship of a single, supreme God whose name is Yahweh. So the question that arises is did this change with the New Testament? Did Christ's coming down to earth change the arrangement made between God and us? Did Christ usurp Yahweh's power? Does he now share it? Finally, was Jesus on earth really just Yahweh (God) in human form?

To find out the answers to all of these questions we should go right to the source. After all, for us

Christians Jesus should be not only our savior and namesake, but also our teacher. He should be the inspiration for how we handle all our daily affairs. Jesus, in fact, told us he was to be our only teacher in regard to spiritual matters.[72] So who better to explain the divine relationships found in the Bible than Jesus? If we truly choose to follow in Christ's footsteps it makes sense to know as much as we can about him, his beliefs and his teachings. In keeping with the previous chapter's theme let's start with his name.

You say you're a friend of whom?

> *The woman said, "I know the Messiah is coming—the one who is called Christ. When he comes, he will explain everything to us." Then Jesus told her, "I am the Messiah."*
> John 4:25-26

Obviously, English speaking Christians know the name of Jesus Christ. However, many aren't aware that this is his English name, just as my name is the English equivalent of Antonio, my father's Italian middle name. Most people aren't aware of its Hebrew origin or how it was originally pronounced. Jesus Christ's name in its original language is *Yashua ha Mashiach*; and, as is common with the vast majority of names found within the Bible, *Yashua ha Mashiach* has a profound meaning.

Let's begin with Yashua, or the more common spelling of Yeshua,[73] which means *Yahweh's Salvation* or *Salvation from Yahweh*. This is why Paul said that God gave Jesus the *"name above all other names."*[74] What could be a more fitting name for the one who left his

Father in heaven, to come down and gave his life as a ransom for all of mankind? With that said, Yeshua was a very common Hebrew name. In fact, the name Yeshua appears in the Old Testament nearly thirty times under different uses. It had been used as a Hebrew name long before Jesus' time on earth.[75] On the other hand, the name Yahweh only refers to the God of the Israelites in the Bible.

Another question that needs to be addressed is how the Y turned into a J. First, there isn't an equivalent sound in classical Hebrew for the soft g sound we have for the j in our modern English language. To be clear, the *jh* sound didn't exist in Hebrew. The same goes for ancient Greek and Latin.

Before the 14th century there wasn't a language that even contained the letter j. It began its life as a fancy i. It was used alongside i in Roman numerals when more than one i was required, e.g. the number 23 would be written xxiij instead of xxiii. In fact, the letter j was only used as a Roman numeral in the first edition of the King James Bible. Names such as Jacob and Jesus were spelled Iacob and Iesus respectively, with the i having the consonantal sound of the y in yellow. Then the j started to be used in the same manner as the letter i, when i was used as a consonant. Again, in this case they both still had a sound similar to the y as in yellow. It wasn't until the 17th century that j had become more widely used, but still not in the way that it is used today.

The sound change from *yah* to *jah* happened as a natural evolution within the Latin language; the pronunciation of words which began with the *yah* sound naturally evolved into the *jah* sound. These types of changes aren't uncommon. As an example, we can hear the results of such changes in the different dialects of English in the United States, Australia, and Great Britain. In fact, with all of its dialects, you can see this within the borders of the United States itself.

This brings us to our Savior's name and its modern pronunciation. The first English speaking Christians had been introduced to it by people who spoke Latin; only, it was the Latin that had changed over the years. The new converts had no way to know the correct pronunciation of Hebrew words such as Jerusalem and Joshua, was, in fact, *Yah*rusalem and *Yah*shua, respectively. It wasn't until classical Hebrew was actually studied by English speaking biblical scholars centuries later that the errors were discovered. By that time the language was thoroughly understood the pronunciations that we have today were already firmly imbedded into our language. Incidentally, these reasons, the deliberate mispronunciation of the divine name and the history of the j sound, are why we have the incorrect but common transliteration of Yahweh into Jehovah.

One final note on the modern spelling of Jesus: the s was added on the end as the result of the rules of Greek syntax. Greek masculine names usually end with a consonant, with the letter s being the one most used for the task. As a result, we have the s at the end of his name completing the evolution of *Yashua* to *Jesus*.

Now, what about mashiach?

I'm glad you asked.

The English equivalent of mashiach (which is Hebrew for *anointed* or *chosen one of God*) is messiah. The terms Christian and Christianity both stem from Christ, which, in turn is derived from *Khristós*. *Khristós* is simply Greek for *anointed.* While this title is most associated with Jesus there were other men in the Bible called messiah. One notable example would be Cyrus, the Persian king who released the Israelites from Babylonian bondage. Yahweh himself referred to Cyrus as *"his anointed one."*[76]

Even though the title of messiah had been previously used in the Bible (as was the name Jesus), the resurrection of Jesus confirmed that he was *the* messiah, as foretold in Jewish scripture. From the point of view of Christians, all the various names: Jesus Christ, Jesus the Messiah and Yashua ha Mashiach now refer exclusive to their namesake. Jesus Christ is the long awaited messiah that the prophets spoke of in Jewish scripture. But what exactly does this mean? Are there really scriptures that foretold of his arrival? Of his crucifixion? Of his place in heaven before and after his time on earth?

Absolutely.

There are quite literally hundreds of prophetic Jewish scriptures that emphatically point to Jesus. From his time with Yahweh before the earth was formed, to the day when he will return to reclaim it from Satan, Jesus' life has been prophetically foretold in all its glorious detail. There have been many books written on the subject. Additionally, I assume that since you're reading this book you already believe in Jesus, his ministry, his performance of miracles, his crucifixion, and his resurrection. Consequently, we won't go into the subject with any great detail. After all, this book is not about whether or not he existed, nor is it about the veracity of the claims about him found within the Bible.[77]

However, since this chapter is all about Jesus' teachings we will review Jewish scripture whenever he referred to them. This is necessary to show the foundation on which his ministry was built.

Now, let's start from the beginning… of the New Testament.

The Good News

> *[Mary] will have a son, and you are to name him Jesus, for he will save his people from their sins.* Matthew 1:21

> *This is the Good News about Jesus the Messiah, the Son of God.* Mark 1:1

> *You will conceive and give birth to a son, and you will name him Jesus. He will be very great and will be called the Son of the Most High.* Luke 1:31-32

> *I saw the Holy Spirit descending like a dove from heaven and resting upon him… I saw this happen to Jesus, so I testify that he is the Chosen One of God.* John 1:32, 34

If we truly want to learn about Jesus we should start with the first four books of the New Testament known as the gospels (good news) of: Matthew, Mark, Luke and John. The gospels are the most direct connections to Jesus' life and teachings. His parables and sermons are told in the first person, with the gospels corroborating each other as to the general facts. It is in them that Jesus is directly quoted most often. Consequently, they are our primary source of his teachings. They're our most solid link to Christ himself.

Tradition has it that Matthew and John are essentially the eyewitness accounts of two of his original Apostles, while Mark was believed to be written by a friend of the Apostle Peter, and Luke was written by a friend of Paul. Mark is believed to be the first gospel written (around 55 A.D.) while John (around 95 A.D.) is believed to be last. The first three are also called synoptic gospels because of the striking similarities between them. They all chronicle the life of Jesus from basically the same perspective, with the intent of recording the life of Jesus; while the more poetic gospel of John, in many ways, stands apart from the others.

These four books by far most illuminate Christ's life. However there are others which bring additional information about Jesus and the early church. For instance, besides the four gospels two other books of the New Testament quote Jesus, just not in respect to his earlier ministry. We learn from the Acts of the Apostles that the resurrected Jesus spoke to his disciples about their coming baptisms by way of his Father's spirit.[78] We also learn in Acts about the confrontation between Jesus and a Pharisee named Saul concerning his persecution of Christians, which would lead to his subsequent conversion to Christianity.[79] Over time Saul, otherwise known as Paul, had several visions of Jesus which guided his evangelizing.[80]

The book of Revelation is a vision of a prophecy of God, which was revealed to the author, John of Patmos, by Jesus through an angel. After a brief introduction, Jesus addressed the problems of seven churches in the province of Asia (present day western

Turkey). He gave encouragement to those who were suffering because of their devotion, and warned of condemnation for those who had strayed from the path of his teachings and remained non-repentant.

There are many other books and letters, including other gospels, written during the early time of the church's history that didn't make it into the Bible; nonetheless, they give additional insight to Jesus and his early followers. We can learn through these other writings much about the lives and ministries of the Apostles and other early Christians, of their martyrdom, and of the early church in general. These texts, along with the books found within the New Testament, were hand copied and passed between the various followers of Jesus, and between the different churches which were springing up after his death. For centuries all of these individual texts about Christ and his followers were shared independent of each other. However, of the hundreds of writings and letters which existed, 27 were eventually selected and canonized by the leaders of the Orthodox Church to form the New Testament. And since Christ's story as found within the Bible is our primary concern here we will stick to those books and letters found within it.

The not so early days

> *The Word became human and made his home among us. He was full of unfailing love and faithfulness. And we have seen his glory, the glory of the Father's one and only Son.* John 1:14

There isn't much recorded in the Bible about the early years of Jesus Christ while on earth. The events of his divine conception and birth are outlined only in the books of Matthew and Luke, as are some of the prophecies which were fulfilled with his arrival. Mark and John, however, start their gospels with the baptism of Jesus by John the Baptist.[81] This would lead us to believe that the years prior to this were relatively inconsequential. However, there is one story in Luke about Jesus as a child that gives us some insight as to his awareness of his own lineage.

Joseph and Mary had lost track of Jesus during their yearly pilgrimage to Jerusalem for the Passover celebration. They finally found him in the temple of Yahweh talking with religious leaders. Surprised at their concern Jesus remarked, *"Didn't you know that I must be in my Father's house?"*[82] This is the first indication that we have from Jesus that he was aware of his time with his heavenly Father before he became human, but not the last. As an adult Jesus spoke often of this earlier time with Father because it is pivotal in understanding the true extent of his sacrifice. For instance, Jesus announced several times that he was sent from God;[83] talked of things he saw and heard when he was with God;[84] prayed to God to bring him back into the glory they formerly shared before the existence of the earth;[85] clearly laid out his chronology to his disciples.[86]

As we can see from these scriptures Jesus had an existence prior to his time on earth. It was during this earlier time that God made all things through him.[87] However, this doesn't mean that we should automatically assume that Jesus was either eternal or equal to God. In fact, the Bible tells us that Jesus was God's firstborn of all creation, which actually leads us to the opposite conclusion.[88] Furthermore, we will soon find out the words of Jesus will unequivocally affirm that their heavenly relationship is the same hierarchal, father-son type relationship that exists between a father and son here on earth. Incidentally, Luke sums up Jesus' early years simply by saying that Jesus grew "*in favor with God.*" Years later Jesus reaffirmed this, announcing that "*God the Father has given me the seal of his approval.*"[89]

The reason we know so little about the early years of Jesus is that his ministry didn't truly begin in earnest until after his baptism by John. This is when Jesus was subsequently filled with the spirit of God. The synoptic gospels all record that the heavens opened up and God's spirit descended on him *"like a dove"* as God declared that Jesus was his "*dearly loved son.*" [90] The next day John the Baptist confirmed that the event took place, rightly concluding that Jesus was the *"Chosen One of God."*[91] Some time later John's disciples questioned him about Jesus' right to baptize. John once again explained that Jesus was sent by God; that through God's limitless spirit Jesus spoke God's words; and this was because "*Father loves his son.*"[92] It was only after Jesus was filled with God's spirit that he was ready to begin spreading the Good News of God's Kingdom. Finally, Luke wrote that *"Jesus was about thirty years old when he began his public ministry."*[93] The baptism story showed the absolute necessity of Yahweh's endorsement of Jesus and of his ministry on earth; Jesus was powerless without his Father's seal of approval.

As this chapter is all about Jesus, for the remainder of it, with very few exceptions, we will only refer to those scriptures in which Jesus is being quoted, or to the Old Testament scriptures to which he referred. We will learn straight from his own words who Jesus claimed to be, what he taught, and why he came. We will also learn what Jesus asked of his original followers. In this way, there can be little confusion on what it means to be a true follower of Jesus. With that said, let's start with who Jesus claimed to be.

The Chosen One

I am the Messiah. John 4:26

Earlier in this chapter we briefly touched upon the biblical use of the Hebrew and Greek titles *messiah* and *christ*. We learned that they both mean *anointed one.* We also learned that, although they had been used in the past referring to other people in the Bible, they had become synonymous with the name of Jesus. In other words, whenever they are used in the New Testament, they refer only to Jesus. The next question that needs to be answered is what it means to be the messiah.

Throughout most of their history, the Israelites had been under the oppressive dominion of one foreign ruler after another. For centuries Israel was subjugated, in chronological order, by the: Egyptians, Assyrian, Babylonian, Persian and Grecian Empires. And for centuries Israel's prophets had been heralding the arrival of a messianic figure that would free them from their bondage, and restore the nation of Israel to its former glory.[94]

By the start of the 1st century Jews had once again been living under just these conditions. For many decades the entire region, and most of the known world, had come under the brutal control of the Roman Empire, which was at the apex of its power. To Rome, Jerusalem was just a small, insignificant town in a backwater province, on the fringe of their empire. To the Jews, Rome was just another in a long line of oppressors that ruled with an iron fist. The Jewish people had been desperately waiting for their messiah to come and fulfill all of the biblical prophecies that had been handed down from generation to generation. They believed he would conquer their Roman oppressors and usher in the age of a New Jerusalem. The time was right for their messiah to arrive.[95]

It was under these conditions that Jesus started his ministry; part of this ministry was his claim that he was the hoped for messiah. Early on, while Jesus was visiting the synagogue in his home town of Nazareth, he read from the scroll of Isaiah, *"The Spirit of [Yahweh]... is upon me, for he has anointed me to bring Good News to the poor.*[96] He then handed back the scroll and proclaimed, "*The Scripture you've just heard has been fulfilled this very day!"*[97] This was the first indication from Jesus that he was, in fact, the messiah. Jesus often alluded to his identity in this manner; by recalling scripture. For instance, while referring to himself Jesus quoted Psalm 118:22-23 to some irate religious leaders, *"The stone the builders rejected has now become the cornerstone. This is [Yahweh's]... doing and it's wonderful to see."*[98]

One day Jesus asked his disciples who they thought he was. Peter answered: *"You are the Messiah, the Son of the Living God,"* to which Jesus responded,

"You are blessed... because my Father in heaven has revealed this to you."[99] Jesus also told his disciples (referring to himself) that they had *"only one teacher, the Messiah;"*[100] and knowing that his work on earth was not yet finished, Jesus warned his disciples several times not to tell anyone what he revealed to them regarding his identity.

On yet another occasion, while he was in Jerusalem for the holy days, Jesus was confronted by some Jewish leaders who claimed he was breaking the laws of the Sabbath. Once again, alluding to who he was, Jesus said, *"You search the Scriptures because you think they give you eternal life. But the Scriptures point to me!"*[101]

Finally, while teaching in the temple, alluding to himself Jesus referred to Psalm 110 declaring that he would be seated in the place of power at the right hand of Yahweh. This Psalm is a messianic prophecy in which Yahweh tells of the wonderful plan that he has in store for his messiah.[102]

Interestingly, the first person to whom Jesus actually told he was the messiah was a Samaritan woman of ill repute.[103] The Samaritans worshipped Yahweh and many of their religious customs were quite similar to Judaism but they disagreed with the Jews as to where he should be worshipped; the Samaritans built their temple to Yahweh on Mount Gerizim while the Jews built their temple in Jerusalem. The two groups were often at odds with each other. As a result, they seldom, if ever, associated. In fact, to the Jews a Samaritan was a second class citizen, with the very name Samaritan being considered derogatory and insulting. There were definite hostilities between them, so when Jesus was called a

"Samaritan devil" by an unbeliever, it was meant to be very demeaning.[104] Nevertheless, Jesus chose to reveal himself to this woman first to show the equality of all people in the Kingdom of God; God's gift of life is for everyone.[105] Jesus used Samaritans in some of his parables for this very same reason-and to teach us to love our enemies.

Eventually, during a mock trial Jesus was asked by the high priest if he was the messiah, the son of God. Jesus acknowledged that it was so.[106]

This sealed his fate.

If the Jewish religious leaders and high council, known as the Sanhedrin, didn't accept Christ's claims he would be accused of blasphemy.

They didn't and he was. [107]

In hindsight, it is very easy for us to see that Jesus was the true messiah; but at the time he was just one of many individuals who claimed that same title. Jesus was well aware of this. In fact, he warned his disciples several times not to be misled by anyone else claiming to be the messiah.[108] Jesus knew that the veracity of his claim-that he was the *Chosen One* of God-hinged on his actions, as he himself said: *"I have a greater witness than John—my teachings and my miracles. The Father gave me these works to accomplish, and they prove that he sent me... the proof is the work I do in my Father's name."*[109]

This brings up several questions: to whom did Jesus refer when he spoke about Father? Did he really think that he was *the* son of God, or was he just being metaphorical? And, most importantly, did he ever claim to actually be the Almighty God described in the Jewish

Bible? Let's find out through his own words what Jesus taught.

The dearly loved son

> *I assure you that the time is coming, indeed it's here now, when the dead will hear my voice—the voice of the Son of God. And those who listen will live.* John 5:25

Throughout his time on earth Jesus referred to God as Father, not only in the general terms of *our Heavenly Father,* or *the Father,* but also as his personal Father.[110] And while Jesus said we are all considered *children of God* he also claimed many times to be the *chosen son of God*; a son with a special relationship reserved only for him.[111] An excellent example of this is found in one of the most often quoted scriptures in the Bible:

> *For God so loved the world that He gave His only begotten Son, that whoever believes in Him should not perish but have everlasting life.* John 3:16 NKJV

Jesus consistently interchanged the terms Father and God. To him they were one and the same expression for describing Yahweh. This we know because of what Jesus said in Luke 2:49 and John 2:16, in which he referred to the temple in Jerusalem as his *"Father's house."* The temple was built by King Solomon for Yahweh and under the direction of Yahweh.[112] Every Jew would know this and would understand the personal connection Jesus was making with him. They would also clearly understand that whenever Jesus talked about his god he would always be referring to Yahweh; since the time of Abraham Yahweh had been considered to be the only true god of the Jews.

When a devout 1st century Jew referred to his own god as *God*, he always meant Yahweh. We will see in the next chapter that, almost without exception, whenever the disciples of Jesus spoke the word God they were also exclusively referring to Yahweh. We will also find out that, almost without exception, they referred to Jesus as lord, teacher or messiah. They didn't call Jesus god because they didn't believe he was Yahweh.

This point must very be clear.

The disciples never, ever thought Jesus was God.

And why didn't they?

Jesus never claimed to be God.

Never.

He always claimed to be the *son of God*.

Incidentally, Jesus wasn't the only one that knew he was the son of God. Remember Peter's answer to the question Jesus posed regarding his identity? Peter replied, *"You are the Messiah, the Son of the Living God."*[113] So, Peter also believed Jesus was the *son of God*. About a week later Peter, along with James and John, were given the ultimate confirmation of this revelation from none other than Yahweh himself. It was during Jesus' famed transfiguration.[114] As they looked on Jesus' physical appearance had changed until his face glowed like the sun. Suddenly Elijah and Moses appeared and began to converse with Jesus. Then a voice boomed from a cloud that had overshadowed them all: "*This is my dearly loved Son, who brings me great joy. Listen to him."*[115]

It wasn't just the good guys who recognized the difference between Father and son; demons acknowledged this as well. A great example of this occurred while Jesus visited the region of Gerasenes, where he confronted a demon possessed man in a cemetery who yelled "*why are you interfering with me, Jesus, Son of the Most High God? In the name of God, I beg you, don't torture me*!"[116] It's ironic that the demon resorted to invoking God while pleading with Jesus for mercy. This also happened in a synagogue in Capernaum where another demon possessed man shouted *"why are you interfering with us, Jesus of Nazareth? Have you come to destroy us? I know who you are—the Holy One sent from God!"*[117]

We learn from Luke that this was quiet a common occurrence: "*Many were possessed by demons; and the demons came out at his command, shouting, "You are the Son of God!"*[118] Demons have, by their very nature, a more intimate understanding of the divine realm than humans; after all they were once angels. So it makes absolutely perfect sense that they would recognize the son of God when they saw him. Consequently, it's a noticeable problem for Trinitarians that no demon ever referred to him as God. As for their ruler, the prince of the demons, we've seen that Satan tried to use Jesus' position as the son of God to tempt him into sin.

There was an incident in Jerusalem which proves that Jesus never claimed to be God. Jesus was surrounded in the temple by a mob that was going to stone him for blasphemy because they incorrectly believed that he claimed to be God. In his response to the accusation Jesus quoted Psalm 82:6:

> *It is written in your own Scriptures that God said to certain leaders of the people, "I say, you are gods!" And you know that the Scriptures cannot be altered. So if those people who received God's message were called "gods," why do you call it blasphemy when I say, "I am the Son of God"?*
>
> John 10:34-36

Here we have Jesus nicely clarifying his stance. Rather than claiming to be God, Jesus insisted that he only claimed to be the son of God. He also made an excellent point about the use of the word god; as we've learned, it isn't only used to describe the Almighty God. Jesus was questioned as to his identity on yet another occasion in Jerusalem. This occurred on what would be the final day of his life. Brought before the high council of Jewish leaders, he was asked directly if the rumors they had heard were true. Was he claiming to be the son of God? Here was the ultimate opportunity to clear the air once and for all. Yet instead of denying it, depending on the gospel quoted the response Jesus gave was either, "*you have said it,*" "*I am,*" or "*you say that I am.*"[119]

Of the many chances Jesus had to accept the helm of God he never took it. With one exception, which we will address later, he always clarified and corrected anyone who mistakenly referred to him as God, or whoever inferred that Jesus himself claimed it.

Jesus never claimed to be God.

He was clear as to his own identity, an identity that has never changed. Jesus has always been, and will always be the *son of God.* This title, incidentally, is actually one that has been bestowed upon angels and upon mankind many times in the Bible. Although Jesus claims this title often, to God, we are also considered *sons of God* (*children of God* in certain translations), as are the angels. In as much as the earthly Jesus was *of God*, so are the angels and those of us that follow in Christ's ways. [120] Jesus' use of the title, however, was meant to connect him to the role of messiah, which would have been understood by his Jewish followers … and by his opponents.

As a side note, Jesus equated himself with another title in the Bible that his fellow Jews would have recognized immediately. On several occasions Jesus called himself the *son of man* and proclaimed that the he would return on clouds from heaven. In this prophecy, taken directly from the book of Daniel, the *Ancient One* symbolizes Yahweh and the *son of man* represents his messiah.[121] So here again rather than being God, we have Jesus placing himself in the role of God's messiah. This is the crux of the issue: by claiming to be the messiah, or the son of God, or the son of man, Jesus had thrust himself into center stage as the pivotal figure for the hope of Jews, and indeed, all of mankind.

This brings up a couple more questions: what did Jesus think about the nature or essence of his relationship with Father? Did Jesus believe, as Trinitarians insist, that he was God's equal? Let's find out, again, through the words of Jesus.

A chip off the ol' block!

> *I live because of the living Father who sent me.* John 6:57

As a good son should be, Jesus was extremely proud of his Father, and of their close relationship. Jesus pulled no punches about this connection. In fact, it can be summed up with one sentence, *"The Father and I are one."*[122]

That's pretty close.

Jesus made other such similar statements, such as: *"the Father is in me, and I am in the Father," "If you had really known me, you would know who my Father is,"* and *"I am not alone because the Father is with me."* [123] Do these scriptures imply that Jesus and Yahweh are both actually different names for the same, single god, as some propose? Or do they show that, while they are separate beings, they are in the big picture equal to each other?

Neither is the case.

These scriptures all wonderfully illustrate the extreme level of intimacy that exists between Yahweh and Jesus. They show that the bond that Jesus has with his Father is palpable. Once again, it comes down to context.

Without keeping within the context of the chapters, or the books, or the overall theme of Christ's teaching, virtually anything can be taught and backed up with scripture. This has, in fact, been going on for centuries. For instance, Jesus once declared, *"Don't imagine that I came to bring peace to the earth! I came not to bring peace, but a sword."*[124] Does this mean we should go on Holy Wars against other religions? Or does this mean that it's open season on suspected witches? Maybe Jesus is telling us we should eliminate any and all Christians that disagree with us. With the scripture taken out of the context of Jesus' overall philosophy, all of the above scenarios are plausible, and all have happened.

Obviously, I don't think Jesus meant that we should have done any of the above. He was speaking figuratively, as he was so prone to do. We can we be sure of this by the overwhelming majority of times that Jesus denounced violence; and by the passivity of his first followers as they went to their deaths on his behalf. More importantly, we can read the scriptures immediately prior to the one in question and see that Jesus was preparing his followers for everything up to and including their own family turning on them. He candidly told them they would be "*sheep among wolves*."[125] Sheep are not exactly known for their aggressive behavior.

The truth of the matter is that Jesus, by his own admission, spoke often in parables.[126] He also used metaphors, similes and all other figures of speech. On various occasions Jesus called Peter Satan; said that he came for God's lost sheep; that the earth would have labor pains; that the disciples would fish for men; and that we should all take up crosses.[127] Should these statements be taken figuratively or should we stop what we're doing and go to a lumber yard? The above scriptures show that Jesus can't always be taken literally. In fact, he spoke in metaphors as often as not. That's why we must take into consideration Christ's overall philosophy and message when discerning between a literal and metaphorical interpretation.

Let's get back to the question posed above: are Yahweh and Jesus different expressions of the same, single God as some denominations assert? If this is so he sure went to great lengths to conceal the truth from us. While on earth Jesus continually referred God as his Father who *is* in heaven; said at least ten times that it was Father who sent him to earth; said that he *"came from the*

Father into the world," and *"would leave the world and return to the Father;"* and even used his heavenly Father as a witness to satisfy the requirement of the Jewish law that states *"if two people agree about something, their witness is accepted as fact. I am one witness, and my Father who sent me is the other."*[128] Finally, Jesus said to *"trust in God, and trust also in me."*[129]

Question one: to whom was Jesus referring?

Jesus prayed often, both publically and privately.[130] During one such time he made a particularly insightful comment while praying over the dead body of Lazarus. He looked towards the heaven and said, *"Father, thank you for hearing me. You always hear me, but I said it out loud for the sake of all these people standing here, so that they will believe you sent me."*[131] Jesus made another interesting comment the night before his arrest. He prophetically confronted Peter as to his soon to be wavering faith, stating that he *"pleaded in prayer"* that Peter's faith wouldn't falter.[132] Finally, while suffering on the cross, Jesus cried out, *"My God, My God! Why have you abandoned me?"*[133]

Question two: to whom was Jesus speaking?

God also spoke about Jesus, once when he was baptized and once during his transfiguration. In both cases he called Jesus his *"dearly loved Son."*[134] John the Baptist confirmed the first incident;[135] while, Peter confirmed the details of the transfiguration in his second letter: *"We saw his majestic splendor with our own eyes when he received honor and glory from God the Father.*

The voice from the majestic glory of God said to him, "This is my dearly loved Son, who brings me great joy."[136]

Question three: who in heaven was doing the talking?

Unless Jesus and God are, in fact, two separate beings as the above scriptures suggest, a fourth question naturally arises: was Jesus a schizophrenic ventriloquist? What would be the point of creating this huge façade of a father-son relationship if there was only a single God? Why would God build a ministry on a fabrication? Finally, why would the God who continually condemned humans to death en mass, enforcing the sentence at least twice, allow *himself*, or even an expression of himself (as some people euphemistically believe) to be tortured and crucified for these very same humans?[137]

There answer is obvious. He wouldn't.

Taken into consideration all of the above scriptures it seems apparent that the only plausible scenario is that Yahweh and Jesus are two separate and distinct beings. We have Yahweh our God, and Jesus, his son. While there are some who would argue that this is too simplistic an understanding there is absolutely no reason to believe that the above scriptures shouldn't be understood in their simplest terms. The messages found within the Bible are intended for us. Hence it stands to reason that the easiest interpretation is the correct one. Jesus, in fact, thanked God for revealing his kingdom to the *"childlike."*[138] We will learn what the disciples had to say in greater detail a little later, but it is worth noting here something that Paul wrote:

> *My message and my preaching were very plain. Rather than using clever and persuasive speeches, I relied only on the power of the Holy Spirit. I did this so you would trust not in human wisdom but in the power of God.* 1st Corinthians 2:4-5

Considering that he penned a large portion of the New Testament, these words of Paul are quite insightful. This holds true with the Old Testament as well, as a hymn to Yahweh reveals, *"The teaching of your word gives light, so even the simple can understand."*[139] The Bible only becomes confusing when "proof" has to be fabricated for manmade doctrines such as the Trinity. This is exactly the time when you need to have your guard up, because so-called theologians will step in and try to convince you that certain scriptures don't actually mean what their obviously stating. It is one thing to acknowledge when a person is using a metaphor to illustrate a point; it's quite another to disregard the actual and explicit meaning for a distorted one simply for the sake of garnering "proof." Yahweh warned that this would happen through the prophet Isaiah.[140] Jesus agreed, reciting the scripture to some Pharisees and religious teachers, *"These people honor me with their lips, but their hearts are far from me. Their worship is a farce, for they teach man-made ideas as commands from God. For you ignore God's law and substitute your own tradition."*[141]

How can one be sure that this book isn't doing exactly what it claims others have done? Michael Shermer, founder and editor of "Skeptic Magazine" rightly suggests that the first rule of skepticism is to question the skeptic. Accordingly, the proof of what this book asserts is not in this book; it is found in the scriptures themselves. The most obvious understanding of a verse is undoubtedly the correct one; scripture like the vast majority of other books, speaks for itself. And while it is true that tradition may get the benefit of doubt it doesn't presuppose its irrefutability. It is impossible to accept the Bible in its entirety and come to the conclusion of Trinitarians without doing incredible feats of linguistic and theological calisthenics.

Incidentally, we just scratched the surface here in regard to the father-son relationship of Jesus and Yahweh. The gospels, as well as the rest of the New Testament books are filled with scriptures that reinforce this relationship. At the same time they're sorely lacking any credible evidence to substantiate the concept of a single God consisting of two (or three, counting the holy spirit) beings. The scriptures that are used as "proof" for this doctrine are scant, taken out of their original context, and taken out of the context of the overall theme of the Bible. It is for reasons such as these that you will hear from the pulpit, radio or television something to the effect that the word of God is far too complex for our feeble minds to comprehend; or that we need some sort of elite priesthood to be the translator of the divine word for us.

This is categorically untrue.

First of all, Jesus told his disciples very clearly that they were all equal in the eyes of his Father:

> *Don't let anyone call you 'Rabbi,' for you have only one teacher, and all of you are equal as brothers and sisters. And don't address anyone here on earth as 'Father,' for only God in heaven is your spiritual*

> *Father. And don't let anyone call you 'Teacher,' for you have only one teacher, the Messiah.* Matthew 23:8-10

Second, Jesus has completely supplanted all forms of human intervention between God and humans; not only the priesthood as was required in Judaism, but all forms of clergy, then and now. He ensured that no new system of ritual intercession would ever again become necessary under any circumstance; he has become the middle man between us and God.[142] To approach God we need only to believe in Jesus, which was the point of his ministry. Most Christians are familiar with the first part of John 14:6, *"I am the way the truth and the life."* What is perhaps less familiar is the second half of the scripture, *"No one can come to the Father except through me."* Christ's goal was to get us closer to his Father; to this end he has removed all obstacles that were formerly required, such as sacrifices and religious rituals. The last thing he wanted was for a new hierarchal system of priesthood to rise out of the ashes of the Mosaic Law. Unfortunately, the Orthodox Churches and all of the Protestant offshoots did just that. They have successfully undone the work performed by Christ on the cross.

I implore you, don't take my word for it. Review the scriptures in this book, or better yet, just read the entire Bible. Then you can make up your own mind as to the truth. I can assure you that it is not too difficult or mysterious for you to understand. In fact, all those who accept Christ have become priests in our own right.[143] It stands to reason, then, that God's divine spirit will also be with us while we explore scripture.[144] Just try to suspend any preconceived notions that you have, get on an island, and let the word of God speak for itself.

Let's revisit the scriptures that started this chapter, *"The Father and I are one... The Father is in me, and I am in the Father... If you had really known me, you would know who my Father is... I am not alone because the Father is with me."*[145] When read in their proper places and in their proper context, all of the above scriptures show the closeness of *spirit* between Father and son; they do not suggest at all that they are the same single deity. How can we be so sure that Jesus wasn't being literal? He uses the very same language to define the closeness between his disciples, his Father and himself:

> *When I am raised to life again, you will know that I am in my Father, and you are in me, and I am in you.* John 14:20

> *I tell you the truth, anyone who welcomes my messenger is welcoming me, and anyone who welcomes me is welcoming the Father who sent me.* John 13:20

> *Anyone who accepts your [the disciples] message is also accepting me. And anyone who rejects you is rejecting me. And anyone who rejects me is rejecting God, who sent me.* Luke 10:16

> *Just as you [Father] sent me into the world, I am sending them [the disciples] into the world.* John 17:18

> *Anyone who receives you [the disciples] receives me, and anyone who receives me receives the Father who sent me.*
>
> Matthew 10:40

> *I pray that they will all be one, just as you and I are one—as you are in me, Father, and I am in you. And may they be in us so that the world will believe you sent me. I have given them the glory you gave me, so they may be one as we are one. I am in them and you are in me.* John 17:21-23

If the above scriptures are to be taken literally then we are all a part of the Godhead right along with Jesus. After all, Jesus used the very same language that he used describing the relationship between God and him. So to be contextually consistent, what goes for him goes for his disciples and us as well. What's good for the goose is good for the gander, so to speak. However, the more plausible explanation, and one as equally consistent, is that we are to share the same spirit; we are to be of one accord, with one mindset and one purpose, which is the will of God.

It's all a matter of context.

Incidentally, this explanation correlates with the definition of marriage Jesus gave to the Pharisees when questioned as to the validity of divorce. Referring to Genesis 2:24, Jesus said that *"'the two [man and woman] are united into one.' Since they are no longer two but one, let no one split apart what God has joined together."*[146] We see that Jesus used the same expression to describe the level of intimacy that should exist between husbands and his wives as God did in Genesis. They become one. Obviously, neither Yahweh nor Jesus meant to suggest that the physical beings of a married couple would merge to form a single entity; or that they were always a single being with various expressions or facets. Their intention was to explain an abstract concept in concrete terms. Spiritually speaking, the husband and wife should be of one accord.

Again, it's a matter of context.

It's striking that the holy spirit is conspicuously absent from all of the above referenced scriptures. Effectively, Jesus failed to mention the "third god" of the Trinity in every one of these relational statements, some of which are used today as proof for the very existence of the theory itself. It's quite stunning that scriptures that don't actually encompass all three aspects of the Trinity are enlisted as evidence for the Trinity.[147]

In any case, this brings us to the next big question: did Jesus believe he was his Father's equal? The vast majority of Christians believe in the equality of God the Father, Jesus the son, and the holy spirit because it's taught from the pulpit via the Trinity doctrine. But are they equal? If not, where did the idea originate? It turns out that answering these questions is crucial to unraveling the origins of the Trinity.

Who's the boss?

> *I have come down from heaven to do the will of God who sent me, not to do my own will.*
> John 6:38

Whether or not Jesus is called God or son of God can be deemed semantics (many men have been called both in the Bible). However, whether or not he is Yahweh's equal cannot be brushed aside so readily. It is, in fact, the linchpin to the Trinity doctrine, and to much of modern Christianity. Accordingly, probably no part of this book will bring more controversy than the statement that Jesus is not equal to God. This flies in the face of virtually all mainstream Christian denominations. Nevertheless, it's the truth. And while the concept of their equality isn't exactly new to Christianity, it didn't originate with Jesus.

Jesus never claimed to be God's equal; to the contrary, he consistently taught that he was God's subordinate. The Apostles and other early Christians acknowledged this explicitly in their writings. However, over the years various outside influences corrupted Christ's own teachings to the point that he was eventually elevated far above any position that he claimed for himself. Against everything that Jesus taught, and against everything found in scripture, Jesus became God in the modern sense of the term. This was the last thing Jesus had in mind when he ministered to the masses using Jewish scripture as his guide. How could he?

As we've learned, the entire Old Testament is steeped in monotheism, with Yahweh being the unparalleled Almighty God who reigns supreme. This is absolutely the most important message given to us by God through the prophets. Moses warned his people on the banks of the Jordon to remember that *"[Yahweh]... is God both in heaven and on earth, and there is no other."* [148] Isaiah echoed these very words five centuries later, *"You are my witnesses, O Israel!" says [Yahweh]... "You have been chosen to know me, believe in me, and understand that I alone am God. There is no other God - there never has been, and there never will be.*"[149] Jesus agreed. He could not have been more to the point when asked which commandment was most important;[150] Jesus' response came right from scripture, "*[Yahweh]... is our God, [Yahweh]... alone. And you must love [Yahweh]... your God with all your heart, all your soul, and all your strength.*"[151] Any attempt to dilute this simple truth should be attempted only with great trepidation, as is evident in the warning Jesus gave Satan when he tried to get Jesus to prove he was the son of God. Jesus first cautioned, "*You must worship [Yahweh]... your God and serve only him,*" and followed with, "*You must not test [Yahweh]... your God.*"[152] Once again, Jesus cited scripture referring to his Father. We will explore the efforts of Satan to corrupt Jesus a little later.

First, let's see what Jesus felt (and taught) about his relationship with Yahweh. Either Jesus taught that he was God's equal, or he taught that he wasn't. He wouldn't have left such an important issue up in the air. Trinitarians claim the former; this book asserts the latter. Namely, that Jesus never claimed equality with God; and that he consistently subjugated himself under God. We will see that his subordination to God was, in fact, the prime constituent of his relationship with God. Based on the claims of the Trinitarians, this should be an insurmountable task; however, based on scripture it poses no problem at all.

I expect this book will receive a lot of flak from mainstream preachers, particularly because of the above statement about Christ's inequality with God. At the very least it will be considered blasphemous; many will deem me a heretic for espousing it; some (fundamentalist

Christians) will probably condemn me and anyone who purchases this book to fires of hell. Perhaps, but if the statement is a one way ticket to Hades I will be in good company because it comes from Jesus Christ himself, *"I am going to the Father, who is greater than I am."*[153]

The eyes have it

> *Blessed are the eyes that see what you have seen.* Luke 10:23

Let's begin our review of Christ's relationship with God by finding out why Jesus came to earth in the first place. First of all, we know that Jesus specifically said he came to serve, *not* to be served.[154] However, as we've previously read Yahweh demanded to be served. It is, in fact, the overarching theme of Jewish scripture. We also know that Jesus thoroughly agreed with this because he told Satan as much during his temptation in the wilderness.[155]

This isn't equality. In fact, it's the exact opposite of equality.

We may be jumping the gun here; nevertheless, this does not seem like a very good start for Trinitarians. Perhaps this is an isolated statement that isn't indicative of their true relationship. So let's address the scripture that began the previous section, "*I have come down from heaven to do the will of God who sent me, not to do my own will.*"[156] From this scripture we can ascertain that Jesus believed three things: 1) his Father sent him; 2) he came to do what his Father wanted him to do; 3) his own will was irrelevant. This scripture is also straightforward and to the point but, once again, this may be another aberration. Are there more along the same line? It just so happens that the following scriptures are also in agreement:

> *I tell you the truth, the Son can do nothing by himself. He does only what he sees the Father doing.* John 5:19

> *I can do nothing on my own... I carry out the will of the one who sent me, not my own will.* John 5:30

> *I do nothing on my own but say only what the Father taught me.* John 8:28

> *The Father gave me these works to accomplish, and they prove that he sent me.* John 5:36

> *At my Father's direction I have done many good works.* John 10:32

> *I will do what the Father requires of me, so that the world will know that I love the Father.* John 14:31

These scriptures point to the conclusion that Jesus came to earth to do what his Father had commanded; his own volition was inconsequential. There's more.

Next we come to the night of Christ's betrayal on what would be the last night of his life. Jesus told Peter (who had tried to prevent Christ's arrest), *"Shall I not drink from the cup of suffering the Father has given me?"*[15]

Immediately prior to this Jesus had prayed to God about his coming ordeal. Twice he pleaded, "*My Father! If it is possible, let this cup of suffering be taken away from me. Yet I want your will to be done, not mine... My Father! If this cup cannot be taken away unless I drink it, your will be done.*"[158] Once again, we learn from this prayer that it was God's will, and not his own, that Jesus came to fulfill. This included his crucifixion.

It is also clear that Jesus was sent to earth by God. Many scriptures reinforce this including the oft cited:

> "*For God loved the world so much that he gave his one and only Son, so that everyone who believes in him will not perish but have eternal life.* ***God sent his Son into the world*** *not to judge the world, but to save the world through him.*
>
> John 3:16-17 (Emphasis added.) [159]

Jesus told his disciples on more than one occasion that even the words he spoke weren't his own. This is understood in John 8:28 (listed above), and in the following scriptures:

> *I don't speak on my own authority. The Father who sent me has commanded me what to say and how to say it. And I know his commands lead to eternal life; so I say whatever the Father tells me to say.*
>
> John 12:49-50

> *The words I speak are not my own, but my Father who lives in me does his work through me.* John 14:10

> *Anyone who doesn't love me will not obey me. And remember, my words are not my own. What I am telling you is from the Father who sent me.* John 14:24

> *I have told you everything the Father told me.* John 15:15

> *My message is not my own; it comes from God who sent me. Anyone who wants to do the will of God will know* ***whether my teaching is from God or is merely my own.*** John 7:16-17 (Emphasis added.)

Hold the phone.

By his own words Jesus: was sent by his Father; spoke the words of his Father; did the will of his Father; and was crucified at the behest of his Father. Jesus also said that he couldn't do or say anything on his own, and that it was only at his Father's direction that he did good works. This is not the definition of equality by any stretch of the imagination. There's more.

Jesus, in fact, had much more to say on the subject, such as when a religious leader called him good. On the surface the comment seems innocuous. After all, if nothing else Jesus had to at least be as good as his Father. And in reality the equality of the Godhead depends entirely upon it. Consequently, his response of, "*Why do you call me good? Only God is truly good*" is rather unexpected.[160] The simple statement from an admirer garnered quite an unusual response from Christ. Why would Jesus draw such attention to what amounted to a passing compliment? Why would Jesus, the one person to die sinless before God,[161] bother to say that *only God* is truly good? He wanted to use the opportunity to teach a valuable lesson. He wanted everyone within earshot to know unequivocally that he wasn't claiming to be god. In effect, Jesus is saying here, *Only God is truly good. I'm not truly good; consequently, I'm not God.*

Perhaps Jesus was just being humble. After all, Yahweh did grant Jesus the ability to heal the sick, expel demons and raise the dead.[162] That's pretty good; even godlike. This has to account for something, perhaps even to the point of balancing the scales between them. However, after further review we find that Jesus granted to his disciples the same life given power that Yahweh had given him.[163] It stands to reason that if the power to heal and raise the dead makes Jesus God's equal, then the same should apply for his disciples. Based on the ability to heal and reason the dead Jesus and his disciples are all equal to God; that is, they are all part of the Godhead. Right?

Of course not.

The ability to grant power to another automatically presupposes a hierarchical relationship. Granting my son the right to drive my truck (when he's old enough) doesn't automatically make him co-owner of the vehicle. And while it is very true that God gave Jesus authority to forgive sins,[164] it is also very true that Jesus said only what he was *allowed* to say:

> *I don't speak on my own authority. The Father who sent me has commanded me what to say and how to say it. And I know his commands lead to eternal life; so I say whatever the Father tells me to say.*
>
> John 12:49-50

Yahweh granted Jesus the right to judge the world upon his return.[165] It may be said that this evokes some sort of equality between Father and son if it weren't for the qualifications imposed upon Jesus by Yahweh, "*I can do nothing on my own. I judge as God tells me. Therefore, my judgment is just, because I carry out the will of the one who sent me, not my own will.*"[166] Jesus also openly acknowledged that he was unaware of when he would be returning to carry out said judgment. While discussing the signs of his eventual return with his disciples Jesus added that, "*No one knows the day or hour when these things will happen, not even the angels in heaven or the Son himself. Only the Father knows.*"[167] Nor will Jesus, as he pointed out to his disciples, have the right to decide who goes where in heaven after the final judgment, "*I have no right to say who will sit on my right or my left. My Father has prepared those places for the ones he has chosen.*"[168]

In truth, on his return Jesus will act as a sort of power of attorney for his Father, pronouncing judgment in his stead. What does this mean? Yahweh has given Jesus permission to act on his behalf. And like a power of attorney, Jesus will only be able to perform his duty within the parameters outlined specifically by his Father. This begs the question: if Jesus is his Father's equal why would he need permission to do anything?

The concept of equality between the grantor of power (God), and the grantee of that power (Jesus) defies logic! Even more so if the relationship is between life and death. Can any son ever truly be equal with his own father? Can the created ever be equal with the creator? The obvious answer is no. Accordingly, we need to ask whether or not Yahweh and Jesus really have a father-son relationship in the sense that we understand it.

Paul clearly answered the question when he wrote that Jesus was the *"firstborn of all creation."*[169] The writer of Hebrews also affirmed this;[170] as did the Psalmist when he wrote, *"I will make him my firstborn son, the mightiest king on earth."*[171] More importantly, did Jesus teach that he was created? The short answer is yes. Jesus humbly acknowledged that he lived because of "*the living Father who sent*" him.[172] Jesus also knew that after his crucifixion, his fate would once again be decided by his Father. This is evident by the last words he uttered on the cross, "*Father, I entrust my spirit into your hands!*"[173]

It's fairly difficult to come up with a scenario that shows their inequality better than Christ's death. The future of Jesus the Christ was entirely dependent upon the discretion of God. For a second time Christ's existence was literally in the hands of his Father. If Yahweh had chosen not to resurrect Jesus the crucifixion would have been the end of him. In any case, Jesus was justifiably confident that he would be resurrected and return to his Father, saying as much to his disciples before his death, "*I am going to the Father, who is greater than I am.*"[174] Fortunately, Yahweh had a plan which included his son; Jesus was resurrected and given the seat of power at the right hand of God.[175] This is the final and perhaps the most significant example of the hierarchical relationship they had. Jesus would be at the right hand of God. To some this implies that Jesus is omnipotent (all powerful).

Not so.

God also has a left hand.

What does this mean? It means that Jesus doesn't have control over his Father. Consequently, Jesus is not omnipotent as many mistakenly believe. Only Yahweh is truly all powerful. Yahweh did it all. He created Jesus, told him what to do, where to go, what to say, how to die, and, most importantly, allowed him to live once again. Jesus just came along for the ride.

Years later this was affirmed by Paul. He understood their relationship explicitly, addressing it in a letter to the church in Corinth, in which he clarified exactly how their divine relationship worked:

> *The Scriptures say, "God has put all things under his [Jesus] authority." (Of course, when it says "all things are under his authority," that does not include God himself, who gave Christ his authority.) Then, when all things are under his authority, the Son will put himself under God's authority, so that God, who gave his Son authority over all things, will be utterly supreme over everything everywhere.*
>
> 1st Corinthians 15:27-28

Of course, Jesus said the same thing to Mary, albeit a little more succinctly. After his resurrection he simply told her, *"I haven't yet ascended to the Father. But go find my brothers and tell them that I am ascending to my Father and your Father, to my God and your God."*[176]

These past sections contained an abundance of scripture for a reason. I didn't want to leave any doubt as to where Jesus stood on the subject. He was quite clear as to his mission while on earth and after. I let Jesus tell his story in his own words. After all, Jesus referred to himself as our teacher, so we should take him up on the offer and heed his words. It's much too easy to be misled or misinformed by a priest or preacher, even if they have only the best intentions in mind. Context is often lost on a Sunday morning when scriptures are extracted from the Bible, dissected, pulled apart, and then pasted haphazardly together to be used as the basis of a sermon.

The same thing can happen inside a book. Therefore, as I said earlier, please don't just take my word on it. The best way to get an understanding of the Bible is to read it yourself. I'm confident that if you do you will start to see that the basic principles of the Trinity and Oneness doctrines are simply not rooted in the Bible.

4 Toe-may-toe Toe-mah-toe

I am the true grapevine, and my Father is the gardener. John 15:1

Typically, when talking with a believer of the Trinity doctrine seldom does the conversation get this far. Long before this point is reached one of three things happens: 1) I'm told that it doesn't matter because either way God knows who he is and the rest is semantics, which is a very grown-up explanation for holding one's breath; 2) a book is recommended to me, which is a tremendously polite way of telling me that I'm ill-informed; 3) or it is suggested that I speak to some friend or acquaintance "who is an authority on the subject." I kindly respond by saying that I would be positively delighted to have a conversation with anyone regarding this subject, but if the person is a proponent of the Trinity doctrine that person is no authority.

If per chance the conversation continues, it is about this point that I'm reminded of all the many titles that are applied to both God and Jesus. These titles, I am told, are unmistakable proof that the god of the Old Testament and Jesus are, in fact, one and the same. I just have one thing to say to that: rubbish.

Actually I have much to say. However, disproving some sort of mini conspiracy theory is not my idea time well spent. Why do I compare this endeavor to a conspiracy theory? In taking up the challenge I am forced to prove a negative, that something isn't so. Basically, conspiracy theorists make unproven claims and, quite usually, without a shred of evidence to support the claim. The onus is then put upon the other side to prove the theory isn't true. For instance, a person can make the claim that there are unicorns living in the vast expanse of the Sahara Desert and stick to the assertion unless it is proven to be untrue. But how exactly does one go about proving that there aren't any unicorns in the Sahara Desert? This is fallacious reasoning in its purest form. The correct way around this problem would be for the person making the claim to prove that unicorns do live in the Sahara Desert, not the other way around.

The same can be said regarding the various titles attributed to Jesus. It is true that he had many titles connected to him throughout his ministry and through the prophecies of the Old Testament. It is also true that Jesus used allegories such as *son of man*; *the good shepherd, teacher, the vine* and as *Jacob's ladder* to describe himself. He even once referred to himself as a *gate*.[177] On other occasions Jesus was called *the good shepherd, mighty god, wonderful counselor, Lamb of God* and *High Priest* by other biblical figures. We will see that these names in themselves don't *prove* anything. After all, even though some were also used for Yahweh, many of these same titles were connected to other men in the Bible. We've learned that even the name Jesus was used variously throughout the Bible. The name Yahweh, however, has only one use.

Nevertheless, for the sake of clarification I will indulge the Trinitarians and address the various titles attributed to Jesus. I will go through them one by one to debunk the idea that they help to affirm their theory. I will prove the negative, so to speak. To round out the field I will also add *Alpha and Omega*, *First and Last* and, the most offensive of all, the *I AM*, if only to show how creative interpretation can conjure up evidence for just about anything out of thin air. Let's start with the good shepherd.

God will strike the Shepherd

Jesus referred to himself as the good shepherd three times, claiming that he would act as a heavenly shepherd, separating good people from the bad.[178] Jesus also quoted scripture foretelling his own execution using the same terminology, *"Strike down the shepherd, and the sheep will be scattered,"*[179] Coincidentally, Yahweh was also likened to a shepherd several times. The best example of this comes from one of the most famous scriptures in the Bible: "*The Lord is my shepherd; I shall not want.*"[180] This, we are confidently told by Trinitarians, confirms that they are at least equal to each other if not actually one and the same deity.

This is precisely where the conspiracy theory mindset reveals itself. Rather than showing a legitimate connection in relation to the use of what amounts to a very common word, Trinity defenders insist that the burden falls upon the opposition to prove that one does not exist. Basically, it's guilty until proven innocent. As it happens, there is ample proof against their assertion.

Before we continue, though, I'd like to take a quick detour down illogical alley to show how this type of faulty reasoning can make quite a mess of things. Ezekiel is repeatedly called *son of man* by Yahweh. It is a short leap to conclude that Ezekiel was, in fact, Jesus.[181] Continuing along the same corrupted line of rationale as above, all that remains to be said is, *"Prove that Ezekiel and Jesus weren't the same person! Until you do, they are."* Case closed.

Only Jesus and Ezekiel weren't the same person.

And neither are Jesus and Yahweh.

Let's get back to our shepherds.

Being called shepherd is absolutely irrelevant to our discussion on the Trinity because there are at least a dozen additional shepherds mentioned in the Bible, six of which were spiritual shepherds chosen by Yahweh to lead the Israelites: Moses, Joshua, David, Cyrus, Jeremiah and Zechariah. Even death is likened to a shepherd in the Bible.[182] Why are so many shepherds mentioned? Once again, we need to think of the correct context. There were an awful lot of shepherds around during the centuries in which the Bible was written. The Israelites lived an agrarian existence, which revolved around herds of goats and sheep. Everyone would have understood the connection. Consequently, the analogies make perfect sense.

While this should be enough to dispel the supposed connection, let's go a step further. If we assume that Yahweh and Jesus are either the same, or at least equal, simply because they were both called shepherds then, taken to its logical conclusion, every single shepherd mentioned above are also equal to God. This should be particularly troubling for devout literalists who have drawn direct correlations based solely on titles because, by their rules, even death should be included in this new and improved Godhead.

Again, this should be enough to dispel the supposed connection, but let's go a bit deeper. Yahweh went into great detail about the future of the Israelites through the prophet Ezekiel. Using a similar analogy Yahweh declared the *shepherds* of the Israelites his enemies. Yahweh then announced that he would act as their temporary shepherd, *"I myself will search and find my sheep. I will be like a shepherd looking for his scattered flock."*[183] Yahweh continued by telling how he would tend to the flock until it was healthy again. Then he would pronounce judgment, separating the good from the bad.[184] Finally, Yahweh talked of the future, when his chosen servant would take over the job:

> *And I will set over them one shepherd, my servant David. He will feed them and be a shepherd to them. And I, [Yahweh]... will be their God, and my servant David will be a prince among my people. I, [Yahweh]... have spoken!* Ezekiel 34:23-24

In a nutshell, Jesus would be their shepherd so that Yahweh could go back to being their God. Figuratively speaking, (David and son of David would become titles synonymous with the messiah) Jesus is the eternal shepherd of God's flock. With statements from Jesus such as, "*I am the good shepherd; I know my own sheep, and they know me, just as my Father knows me and I know the Father,"*[185] and, "*God will strike the Shepherd, and the sheep will be scattered,"*[186] he agreed.

Jesus made a distinction between God and the shepherd who is, of course, himself. We know from the Bible that both Paul and Peter agreed with this analogy. Paul, for instance, told the elders in the church of Ephesus to, *"Feed and shepherd God's flock."*[187] Peter said the same in an open letter to several churches to, *"Care for the flock that God has entrusted to you."*[188] Peter continued with the comparison in verse four by calling Christ the *"Great Shepherd."* The writer of the book of Hebrews was also in agreement:

> *Now may the God of peace - who brought up from the dead our Lord Jesus, the great Shepherd of the sheep, and ratified an eternal covenant with his blood - may he equip you with all you need for doing his will.* Hebrews 13:20-21

For those keeping track, Jesus referred to himself as the gate in John's gospel, "*I tell you the truth, I am the gate for the sheep... Yes, I am the gate. Those who come in through me will be saved.*"[189] Well, which is it? Is Jesus the shepherd or the gate? I think it goes without saying that Jesus was speaking figuratively here. And, figuratively speaking, he can be all of the above and then some. Here Jesus was trying to relate that it is only through him that we are able to receive the promised salvation that comes from his Father, *"I, yes I, am [Yahweh]... and there is no other Savior."*[190] From the start of his ministry the message was always the same, "*I am the way, the truth, and the life. No one can come to the Father except through me.*"[191] Thus, Jesus is not only the shepherd; he is the gate…or is it lamb?

My way or the highway…

> *The highway to hell is broad, and its gate is wide for the many who choose that way. But the gateway to life is very narrow and the road is difficult, and only a few ever find it.*
> Matthew 7:13-14

There is another title affixed to Jesus which affirms his position as mediator between God and us; that is the title of *High Priest*. Traditionally the High Priest performed a sacrificial ritual once a year on behalf of Israel. This day, known as Yom Kipper (or Day of Atonement), is a day of penance for sins committed against God. As Yahweh explained, it was to be a day *"when offerings of purification"* were to be made for each Israelite, making them *"right with [Yahweh]... your God."*[192] Without going into detail it suffices to say that before the destruction of the temple the High Priest was Israel's direct link to God. Jesus, however, effectively supplanted the need for a High Priest and, for that matter, the priesthood itself. He has become our eternal High Priest. We first learn of this from Yahweh himself when he prophetically avowed that Jesus would become *"a priest forever in the order of Melchizedek,"*[193] but it is the book of Hebrews which explains the role of Jesus as the eternal High Priest in greatest detail. As High Priest, Jesus is our connection to God.

While we're on the subject of sacrifices, there is another Jewish holiday involving sacrifices which has a strong association with Jesus. As most Christians are aware, Jesus is also known as the *Lamb of God*, *the Passover Lamb*, or simply *the Lamb*. These are particularly important titles because of their implications. What exactly do they designate? The answers have to do with the Passover ceremony. Passover began in Egypt, when the Israelites were told by Yahweh to sacrifice an unblemished lamb. Then the lamb's blood was to be smeared around their doorways to protect those inside the house. The blood was a sign to God not to impose the sentence he levied upon the land of Egypt-death to all firstborn male children and animals. After this tenth and final plague was executed, Pharaoh relented and allowed the Israelites to leave Egypt.[194]

Harkening back to this event, the night before his death Jesus alluded to being the symbolic sacrificial lamb and to his coming crucifixion. Handing his disciples bread, he told them, *"This is my body, which is given for you. Do this to remember me... This cup is the new covenant between God and his people—an agreement confirmed with my blood, which is poured out as a sacrifice for you."* [195] It is no coincidence that Jesus' life was taken during the week of Passover. The crucifixion aside, there were certain, specific requirements as outlined in Exodus 12 that had to be met in order to qualify as the Passover sacrifice. These were not necessarily the easiest requirements to fulfill. To begin with, the entire community had to perform the sacrifice (the people and religious leaders called for Christ's crucifixion[196]); the chosen lamb had to be unblemished (Jesus was considered to be perfect by God[197]); none of its bones could be broken (even though it was customary to break the legs of the crucified none of Jesus' bones were broken[198]); its blood, of course, had to be spilled (Christ's blood was spilled[199]); finally, the lamb had to be completely consumed by morning (Jesus was taken down before nightfall[200]).

We can see from the above scriptures that the death of Jesus corresponded with the requirements set by Yahweh in Exodus. Thus, through his crucifixion Jesus has forever replaced the sacrificial lamb for all who believe in the redemptive quality of this act.[201] This highlights the distinctive hierarchal relationship between

Jesus and Yahweh. We have access to God *through* Jesus the High Priest and we receive salvation from Yahweh *through* Jesus, the Lamb of God. Jesus is both the one offering the sacrifice and the sacrifice.

Now, let's continue with our theme and talk about Jacob's ladder.

Stairway to heaven

Jacob, Abraham's son, once had a prophetic dream. In it he had vision of a staircase (or ladder, as the NKJV Bible happens to translate it) bridging heaven and earth:

> *[Jacob] dreamed of a stairway that reached from the earth up to heaven. And he saw the angels of God going up and down the stairway. At the top of the stairway stood [Yahweh]... and he said, "I am [Yahweh]... the God of your grandfather Abraham, and the God of your father, Isaac."*
>
> Genesis 28:12-13

When Jacob awoke he realized he was on hallowed ground, so he named the place Bethel, which is Hebrew for *house of God*. How does this relate to Jesus? Jesus connected himself to the story. However, rather than equate himself with God, or even with the angels of God, Jesus referred to himself merely as the stairway between heaven and earth, *"I tell you the truth, you will all see heaven open and the angels of God going up and down on the Son of Man, the one who is the stairway between heaven and earth."*[202] Jesus was trying to explain to Nathaniel that he would soon become the new way to approach God. God is standing in heaven and Jesus is the stairway to him. I'm forced once again to underscore a painfully obvious but often overlooked fact in this analogy: Jesus didn't say that he was God, nor did he suggest that he was God's equal, which would have made perfect sense if he believed this was so. Jesus only held that he was the way *to* God. That's it. He phrased this idea more directly at a later occasion, "*I am the way, the truth, and the life. No one can come to the Father except through me.*"[203] He is the way to God; he is the only way to God; but he is not God.

Before we move onto a few of the concocted titles used for Jesus there is another agrarian allegory that we need to address. Jesus compared himself and his followers to a grapevine and its branches respectively to illustrate the interrelational aspect of their existence. Jesus used grapevines for the same reason the shepherd/flock metaphors were used so often; wine was an extremely important agricultural product during the 1st century. Wine mixed with water was the drink of choice for many people simply because the alcohol in the wine acted as an antiseptic, preventing water borne illness. Consequently, there are many literal references and metaphoric uses of grapes, grapevines and wine in the Bible. It made perfect sense, then, when Jesus followed suit and declared, "*I am the true grapevine, and my Father is the gardener... Yes, I am the vine; you are the branches.*"[204] Jesus, *the vine*, goes on to explain that if we, *the branches*, stick with him (so to speak), we would produce fruit abundantly. His Father ensured it. On the other hand, if a branch produced no fruit then it would be severed from the vine and discarded.

Now, here's a nice twist on their hierarchal relationships.

In this parable Jesus is actually closer in form to his followers than to God. Jesus and his followers are considered parts of the same whole (a plant), while Yahweh is the gardener who does the pruning. It's up to the gardener to decide which branches stay or go. Perhaps more importantly it's also entirely up to the gardener to plant the vine in the first place. Once again Jesus openly acknowledged that Father (the gardener) is in charge of the whole operation.

Do you still believe that Jesus taught that he was his Father's equal?

I certainly hope not, but if you do it's understandable. Christianity has been steeped in false teachings for so long it has become virtually impossible to distinguish fact from fiction. While we are on the subject, we should end this chapter by discussing some of the unscriptural conflations of God and Jesus made using, interestingly enough, scripture.

Is this an oxymoron?

As we shall see … not at all.

Who's on first?

These next titles are last gasps in the Trinitarians argument. In reviewing these it becomes readily apparent that defenders of the doctrine are grasping at straws, desperately trying to glean any support for their ill-fated, man-made theory. Common sense shows that they prove nothing. Nonetheless, we'll continue addressing these fallacious, conspiracy theory type arguments. Why? To dispel every possible assertion that Yahweh and Jesus are either the same god, or equal to each other. This first one is a softball. Jesus is called *god* or *mighty god* in a few prophetic scriptures, that is, scriptures that have been retroactively linked to Jesus: Isaiah 9:6 and 10:21 and Psalm 45:6-7. Does this make a solid connection between Yahweh and Jesus?

No it doesn't.

We learned the exact meaning of the word god, along with its many uses, in chapter two of this book. Briefly put, it is not the name of the supreme deity; nor does it automatically imply it. Rather, it is simply an oft used title. Adding mighty before it means little more; many persons, places and things are called mighty (Hebrew: *gibbor*) in the Old Testament. However, being called *God Almighty* (Hebrew: *El-Shaddai*) means everything:

> *And God said to Moses, "I am Yahweh - 'the LORD.' I appeared to Abraham, to Isaac, and to Jacob as El-Shaddai - 'God Almighty' - but I did not reveal my name, Yahweh, to them."* Exodus 6:2-3

Yahweh is called *Almighty* (Hebrew: *Shaddai*; Greek: *pantokrator*) at least sixty other times throughout the Bible. However, it is never used to describe Jesus, or anyone or anything else for that matter. Much like shepherd, mighty is just another common word in the Bible. Incidentally, the Psalmist actually pointed out in a prophetic scripture that Jesus had a god of his own: *"Therefore God [Jesus], your God [Yahweh], has anointed you, pouring out the oil of joy on you more than on anyone else."*[205] It is Yahweh himself, who conferred the honor to Jesus in the first place. Even in this scripture the hierarchy between them is apparent.[206]

Up to now, I've used the same Bible translation throughout this book so as not to appear as if I'm searching for the best version to validate my position. The *New Living Translation* (NLT) has been the almost exclusive source of biblical reference for this book. This is through sheer happenstance. It simply happened to be the version handed to me the first time I visited Pastor Mark's church.

However, it helps to have a variety of translations on hand to do side by side comparisons of scriptures. After all, English was not the original language used by the authors of the books of the Bible (not even the King's English of the Authorized Version as many are inclined to believe).[207] Having multiple translations, including Greek and Hebrew interlinear translations, will help improve comprehension and ensure that biases or discrepancies, if any, will be noticed. The next three titles will be reviewed using several other Bible translations for precisely these reasons.

While we're on the subject, I've noticed that many Christian writers are prone to scripture shop, which to me is suspect. If their message truly is biblical it should transcend all but the most unorthodox translations. Besides, I don't believe there is such a thing as "the most accurate translation." With the exceptions of a few modern, very liberally translated versions such as the *Message Bible*, and the *Contemporary English Version*, the basic principles do not change.

The NLT is a very user friendly Bible. It uses common language and gives alternate scripture translations on the bottom of its pages, which I find is quite helpful. The NLT also informs its readers if there is any conflict between the different early manuscripts used as reference during the translation process. This is good to know because, generally speaking, the older the manuscript the more likely it is to represent the original text. The reason goes back to the manner in which the individual books were originally copied, which was by hand, one letter at a time. As a result, the older the text, the fewer chances there are for scribal errors. It was also very common for scribes to put in their own two cents long after the original was penned in an effort to strengthen or clarify a point within the text.

For instance, the NLT has this note connected to 1st John 5:7: *"A few very late manuscripts add in heaven—the Father, the Word, and the Holy Spirit, and these three are one. And we have three witnesses on earth."* The translators of the NLT chose not to include it because they rightly deduced that the phrase wasn't from the hand of the original author. The modern scholarly consensus is that it was a later scribal addition. Nevertheless, other translations have chosen to include it either for the sake of tradition or to support doctrine. We'll return to this controversial verse later.

For the reasons listed above, it will be necessary in the coming three sections to reference other versions because the majority of them do not agree with the NLT regarding the scriptures in question. Consequently, we will review these scriptures from the various translations. As always, you should decide the truth for yourself, based upon contextual agreement and scriptural alignment within the overall framework of the Bible.

The One and only!

> *You are my witnesses, O Israel!" says [Yahweh]... "You have been chosen to know me, believe in me, and understand that I alone am God. There is no other God - there never has been, and there never will be.*
>
> Isaiah 43:10

The phrase, *"I am the Alpha and the Omega"* occurs only three times in most Bible translations, all in John's Revelation. The King James (KJV) and New King James Version (NKJV) both include the phrase a fourth time. However, most of the other translations agree that it was a later addition to the text. Consequently, they do not include it.

The American Standard Version (ASV) the Darby's New Translation (DNT), the International Standard Version (ISV), the English Standard Version (ESV), the KJV and NKJV all ascribe the first (1:8) and third (22:13) uses to Jesus and the second one (21:6) to God. However, the NLT has the first two going to God, and the last attributed to Jesus. The KJV and NKJV attribute their extra verse (11:11) to Jesus as well. We know this through its red letters, which are meant to distinguish the words of Jesus from the rest of the text. This practice, as we will see, is deceptive in itself.

The majority of the translations presume Jesus is speaking in these scriptures because it supports the Trinity doctrine. However, if each scripture is read in its proper context, we see that it is, in fact, Yahweh talking and not Jesus at all. Here is the first, *"I am the Alpha and the Omega—the beginning and the end," says the Lord*

God. "I am the one who is, who always was, and who is still to come—the Almighty One."[208] Two phrases, *the Lord God* and *Almighty One,* immediately jump out and clarify who is actually speaking. As we've learned in the second chapter, *the Lord God* is an Old Testament title for Yahweh, which correctly translated would read *Yahweh your God.* And up to this point in the Bible *Almighty One* has only been used to describe Yahweh; it is sort of like his divine nickname. Why would this suddenly change? It wouldn't.

To get the proper context for the second instance (21:6) we also need to read the verse that follows it, "*And he [God] also said, "It is finished! I am the Alpha and the Omega—the Beginning and the End. To all who are thirsty I will give freely from the springs of the water of life. All who are victorious will inherit all these blessings, and I will be their God, and they will be my children."* [209] This is a scripture in which the NLT has taken some liberties with its interpretation. This is obvious for three reasons.

First, no other translation connects the phrase uttered by Jesus on the cross (*it is finished*) [210] with the phrase used here. This is subtle, but the tie-in is intended to imply that because the phrase is the same, Jesus must also be the one speaking in Revelation. None of the other translations use the same sentence for both scriptures because the key words are completely different; a form of the word *teleo* is used in John, while in Revelation the word *gegonen* is used. A strong indicator that they are not each other's equivalent is evidenced by the use of *telos* in the same sentence as *gegonen* in Revelation.

The second point is not so subtle. As we've discovered, almost without exception, Jesus is never called god. More importantly, he never said that he would become anybody's god; nor did he ever refer to himself as god; or asked to be called god. Finally, all of the other translations listed have the speaker in verse seven describing a single person; they all end the verse with *"my son"* instead of *"my children"* as in the NLT. For instance:

> *He who overcomes shall inherit all things, and I will be his God and he shall be My son.* NKJV

Which is correct translation, my son or my children? The actual Greek phrase is *autos esomai moi ho huios*. *Autos* denotes a singular pronoun *he*, *esomai* means *will be* or *shall be*, *moi* means *me*, *to me* or *mine, ho* is the definite article *the,* and *huios* means *son*. It seems we have a winner: he shall be my son. This, in fact, makes better sense of the scripture because, as Christians know, the one who overcame is Jesus; he overcame the cross to be resurrected to the right hand of his Father. Thus, after a careful review, it is clear that Yahweh was talking specifically about Jesus, his chosen son.

We have only to use the idea of textual continuity to see that Yahweh was speaking in the third scripture. After all, he was speaking the first two times, common sense dictates that it is him the third time. Just to be sure, though, we should read it in its proper context.

The final chapter of Revelation begins by talking about the throne of God *and* of the Lamb (two separate beings), and that they would reign together forever.[211] Verse six then goes on to explain that *"the Lord God"* (Yahweh) sent his angel to tell his servants what was going to take place in the future, "*Then the angel said to me, 'Everything you have heard and seen is trustworthy and true. The Lord God, who inspires his prophets, has sent his angel to tell his servants what will happen soon.'*"[212] Once again, here is where some liberties have been taken. First, the NLT has needlessly inserted a heading between the sixth and seventh verse: "*Jesus is Coming.*" Then, they treat verse seven as if it was Jesus speaking the entire time. However, once again, if read within the context of verse six it is obvious that Yahweh was speaking:

> *Then the angel said to me, "Everything you have heard and seen is trustworthy and true. The Lord God [Yahweh], who inspires his prophets, has sent his angel to tell his servants what will happen soon." Look, I am coming soon! Blessed are those who obey the words of prophecy written in this book.*
>
> Revelation 22:6-7

The angel was sent by God to tell us of his impending visit. The NLT once again continues in verse twelve and thirteen as if Jesus is speaking, "*Look, I am coming soon, bringing my reward with me to repay all people according to their deeds. I am the Alpha and the Omega, the First and the Last, the Beginning and the End.*"[213] It is obvious from verse six that the Lord God (Yahweh) was speaking in verse seven, and by default, verses twelve and thirteen. This is absolutely in alignment with the overall theme of the Bible that Yahweh is the Supreme, Almighty God. But why did Yahweh choose the phrase alpha and omega in the first place?

Alpha and omega are the first and last letters of the Greek alphabet, so the analogy is supposed to show that Yahweh encompasses all things. Another way to say it is that Yahweh is *"the Beginning and the End,"* a phrase which also occurs in these, and only these three scriptures. While we are at it, we might as well include *"the First and the Last"* since it is also included in these three scriptures. Actually this phrase lends more support that it was Yahweh talking and not Jesus because this last phrase had been previously used; it is found three times in the book of Isaiah. Reviewing them might shed a bit more light on its use in Revelation:

> *Who has done such mighty deeds, summoning each new generation from the beginning of time? It is I, [Yahweh]... the First and the Last. I alone am he.*
> Isaiah 41:4

> *This is what [Yahweh]... says—Israel's King and Redeemer, [Yahweh]... of Heaven's Armies: "I am the First and the Last; there is no other God."* Isaiah 44:6

> *Listen to me, O family of Jacob, Israel my chosen one! I alone am God, the First and the Last.* Isaiah 48:12

Here we have three scriptures each containing the same phrase and in all three instances it is Yahweh speaking. To recap:

1) Yahweh had previously referred to himself as "*the First and Last;*"
2) The phrases "*the Alpha and Omega*" and "*the Beginning and the End*" are just twists on the phrase "*the First and Last;*"
3) Most Bible translations attribute the phrase *Alpha and Omega* to Yahweh at least once, if not twice, in Revelation;
4) The surrounding scriptures in Revelation all overwhelmingly point to Yahweh speaking;
5) Jesus had never previously referred to himself as "*the First and Last;*"
6) Jesus had never previously claimed equality with Yahweh.

After all this, are we supposed to believe Jesus said that he was *"the First and Last,"* or *"Alpha and Omega,"* or *"the Beginning and the End,"* simply because the letters in our Bibles are red? This is the only reason to assume that Jesus, and not his Father, was the speaker. The letters in the Bible are red. [214] This is where the deception caused by red letter Bibles is most apparent. The average reader will in all probability not think beyond the implication and assume that Jesus was speaking.

These phrases are used as "proof" by Trinitarians, to defend their stance that the Father and son are one and the same being, and part of the Godhead. However, other than their assertion that it was Jesus speaking (and, of course, the red letters) there isn't any reason to believe that this is so.

This brings us back to the conspiracy theorists guide to the Bible.

Remember my friend Pastor Mark? Well, I recently had a conversation with him about these particular scriptures. He asked me, *"Could it have been Jesus speaking?"* My reply was, "*Yes. It could have been Jesus."*

It's true, it *could* have been Jesus.

It *could* have been the angel who relayed the message to John.

It *could* have been John, the writer of the book of Revelation.

It *could* have been Santa Claus.

It wasn't.

I can be certain based on the overall context and prior scriptural evidence that it was Yahweh speaking. During this discourse there was one point that had been overlooked by Pastor Mark, and other proponents of the Trinity. Let's, for a brief moment, pretend that Jesus did say some catchphrase that was also attributed to Yahweh. So what? All that it would prove is that Jesus was a good listener, and that he admired and wanted to emulate his Father. Many children try to emulate their dads; and Jesus was no different. Imitation is the sincerest form of flattery. Nevertheless, *trying* to be like someone and actually *being* that someone are two very different things.

That's me!

> *The high priest asked him, "Are you the Messiah, the Son of the Blessed One?" Jesus said, "I AM."* Mark 14:61-62

By now I hope that I've dispelled almost all the theoretical connections between Jesus and Yahweh based on similar names. I say almost because there is one left; it's the ol' I AM. This is the most egregious of all the hypothetical connections. We are to believe that simply because Jesus said *"I am"* this, or *"I am"* that, that he is Yahweh, the God talking to Moses from the burning bush.[215]

For instance, when asked how he could have seen Abraham (since Jesus obviously wasn't old enough) Jesus supposedly replied, *"I tell you the truth, before Abraham was even born, I AM!"*[216] The NLT subtly admits that they've might have taken a few liberties with this one. There is an alternate translation in footnote attached to the scripture in question which reads, *"Or before Abraham was even born, I have always been alive."*

Now, I ask you: which response would have made more sense?

It's difficult to believe that the creator of the universe would use poor grammar to cryptically connect himself to a Jewish scripture when he could have simply come right out and said it. In case you skipped the first few sections of this book I'll catch you up on the scripture in question. During their first encounter Moses asked God for his personal name because it hadn't yet been revealed to the people of Israel. Depending on the translation God's first response was anything from "*I am who I am"* (NKJV); to *"I will be what I will be"* (a notation attached to the verse in the NLT); to *"I am that I am"* (ASV).[217] Curiously, this last one was used extensively by the classic hero figure Popeye the Sailor. Do you think there is some sort of divine connection? Is Brutus (Popeye's arch nemesis) actually Satan? If this sounds sarcastic it's because there is literally no end to the connections that can be made between anything and anybody once common sense and context are ignored. As an example, over the years there has been no end to the number of individuals who have been called the antichrist based on as little evidence as the number of letters in their name … and a grudge.

Here's a question: when asked if he was the messiah, rather than answer with the cryptic *"I am,"* why didn't Jesus just say, "*No, actually I'm God*?" Why make the allusion with a response that is so vague that everyone on earth has probably used it at one time or another? If Jesus was trying to reveal to the world that he was Yahweh, the God of the Jews, he certainly went about it the long way.

There is a principle known as Occam's razor, which loosely explained states that if you have two equally likely solutions to a problem, choose the simplest. Applied here, the understanding would be that Jesus meant what he said when asked by the High Priest if he was *"the Messiah, Son of the Blessed One."*[218] It means that when Jesus said *"I am"* he honestly meant, "*Why yes, I am the Messiah, Son of the Blessed One.*" Correspondingly, it also means that when Jesus said *"I am"* he didn't cryptically mean to infer, "*Actually, no I'm not the Messiah. I'm actually the Blessed One you mentioned, the God mentioned in Exodus 3:14 conversing with Moses. I'm not the Son of God; actually I* ***am*** *God. Thanks for asking!*"

He didn't, infer that he was God because he's not God.

Simple.

If this kind of basic logic is applied to all scriptures they would all make much more sense. For instance:

*If Yahweh said repeatedly that he alone is God, why not take his word for it?
*If Yahweh said that we should remember his name, why don't we?
*Why use every poor excuse in the world to justify forgetting it?
*If Jesus never referred to himself as God, maybe he's not God.
*If Jesus said he is the son of God, perhaps he is.
*If Jesus never asked to be worshipped, why do we?
*If Jesus never said that we are to pray to him, why would we?
*If Jesus said his Father is greater than him, and that we should pray, worship and listen only to his Father, why do mainstream churches keep coming up with excuses not to?
*Why don't we just do what Jesus asked us to do?

The good book speaks plainly and speaks loudly. Rather than trying to fit the scriptures to doctrines such as the Trinity, let the scriptures honestly reveal themselves, unmolested by human biases and agendas. Trust me, their meanings will become apparent.

Actually, don't trust me.

Pick up your Bible and read it. You will see that the Bible makes its own connections. This timeless guide isn't ambiguous on its central tenets. If faulty reasoning and wild inferences need to be applied to justify a particular point of view (i.e. doctrine) then the point of view is faulty.

In the beginning was the Word…

> *Jesus said to the disciples, "Have faith in God."* Mark 11:22

Most Christians assume that Jesus was commonly referred to as god in the New Testament. And on a couple of occasions he was. However, most people would be surprised to learn that it's less than a handful. We could, in fact, count the number of times on one hand with fingers to spare.[219]

Confusion about this stems directly from the Trinity.

Describing Jesus as *God the son* who is an equal partner in the *Godhead* allows for the misapplication of the word *god*. Consequently, it is thought to refer to Jesus as readily as Yahweh. However, it is clear from scripture that the word *God* almost exclusively refers to Yahweh. After his name, it is the second most used designation for Yahweh in the Bible. Every New Testament writer carefully distinguished between *God* and *Jesus* by specifically referring to each individually and by constantly describing the relational aspects between *God* and *Jesus.* So, for instance, we see the phrase *God the Father* quite often in The New Testament, yet we never see the phrase *God the Son*. And by referencing Old Testament scriptures the writers directly link their use of the word *God* to Yahweh. There is no plausible reason to believe that *God* is just another term for *Jesus* in the New Testament; they're not interchangeable. Nonetheless, the crucial distinctions between the two are overlooked simply because it's unsupportive of the Trinity doctrine.

The above confusion notwithstanding, there is one instance of Christ being referred to as *god* that has been dissected, analyzed and argued over for centuries by those on both sides of the Trinity debate. (There are many theological scholars that agree that the Trinity doctrine is fallacious.) The scripture in question is quoted often by Trinitarians as part of their overwhelming proof; and, on the surface this tongue twister may seem to show that the writer believed Jesus was at least equal to, if not actually Yahweh, the Almighty God. Even so, before I go into my reasons for not accepting it as "proof" I'd like to make an observation: should a major tenant of Christianity be hinged on one or two ambiguous scriptures?

I've gone to great lengths in this book, especially in this chapter, to show through scripture the overarching theme of Jesus' teachings. One thing should be abundantly clear after reading the four gospels (and this book): Jesus was never vague. He didn't leave much room for speculation as to his beliefs, his teachings, and his purpose. Jesus continually referred to himself as the son of God, and to God as Father-*his* Father. His Apostles understood this. Further along in this chapter we will see that Jesus also never claimed equality with God. We will see that his Apostles also understood this. So to dismiss the preponderance of evidence just to give credibility to one or two scriptures is absurd.

We will address in greater detail the one dubious scripture that is used to substantiate the Trinity myth a little later. We will attempt to understand why certain scriptures have been ignored by Trinitarians. We will also see how, by trying to bring some sense of validity to their manmade teaching, they've convoluted Christ's message to the point that the only kind of response they can give about it when questioned is, *"The divine mind is just too complex for us humans to understand,"* or, *"We have to take it on faith."*

Faith.

I have faith.

I have faith in our Yahweh, our heavenly Father.

I have faith in the redemptive work of Jesus, the son of Yahweh.

And I have faith that the Bible is meant to give us a better insight into the relationships between Yahweh, Jesus and us. I also have faith that the creator of the universe wouldn't have inspired a manual that was too complicated for us to understand.

Again I ask: what would be the point?

The message of Jesus was ultimately aimed at the uneducated masses. He constantly railed against the established religionists who twisted scripture to their own ends. When questioned about the actions of his disciples by some Pharisees he called the Pharisees hypocrites, quoting Isaiah 29:13, "*Their worship is a farce, for they teach man-made ideas as commands from God."*[220]

Finally, I have faith that the message of Christ is so simple that even a child can understand it. Why? Because Jesus said it was: "*O Father, Lord of heaven and earth, thank you for hiding these things from those who think themselves wise and clever, and for revealing them to the childlike. Yes, Father, it pleased you to do it this way!"*[221]

Try and explain the Trinity doctrine to a child.

Let's return to the topic at hand.

If you're familiar with scripture you've probably figured out that the verse in question is John 1:1, "*In the beginning the Word already existed. The Word was with God, and the Word was God.*" While this scripture is poetic, it is quite: abstruse; arcane; recondite. Or simply put, the verse is unclear. Many may read the first three adjectives and question the meaning of the sentence. However, the forth adjective makes it apparent. It gives the thought better clarity. The second sentence helps to clarify the first sentence. The same occurrence is found in John. In fact, the very next verse, *"He existed in the beginning with God"*[222] lends clarity to the first one. The prologue continues by explaining how Yahweh created everything through Jesus, the point being that the Father and son team worked well together. It has to be noted here that most scholars agree that the first 18 verses of John were a later addition to the gospel. It isn't original to the text. With that aside, the scripture is still vague at best.

As we continue, a second scripture in John has been used by Trinitarians to support the doctrine. This one involved the Apostle Thomas who, once he realized that he was in the presence of the resurrected Jesus exclaimed, "*My Lord and my God!*"[223]

My god.

I'll bet that phrase has never been said out of context before.

Assuming that Thomas wasn't actually invoking both Jesus *and* Yahweh in his exclamation, recall the opening chapters of this book and Jesus' explanation of the use of the term god[224] and one thing should be obvious: biblically speaking, using the word god does not automatically presume Yahweh, *the God* of the Old

Testament. We must also recall that both John and Thomas had been near Peter when he was quizzed by Jesus. They would have heard Peter's response that Jesus was *"the Messiah, the Son of the living God"*.[225] Moreover, Jesus asked them all, not just Peter.[226] Accordingly, John and Thomas would have been acutely aware of the stance Jesus had taken as the son of God. As devout Jews and loyal followers of Jesus neither one of them would have made the mistake of confusing Jesus with God. Consequently, if they called Jesus god it would have been in this frame of reference. Neither would have mistaken Jesus for Yahweh the Almighty God that they worshipped.

As John's gospel progresses it becomes readily apparent that the writer of John understood that Jesus was the son of God and not actually God himself. The author's true belief becomes crystal clear in the closing verses of chapter twenty:

> *The disciples saw Jesus do many other miraculous signs in addition to the ones recorded in this book. But these are written so that you may continue to believe that* ***Jesus is the Messiah, the Son of God****, and that by believing in him you will have life by the power of his name.*
>
> John 20:30-31 (Emphasis added.)

It's fitting to close this chapter with an incident taken from John. It should put to rest any possible belief that Jesus taught that he was God, and along with it, any chance that his disciples believed he was God. Jesus appeared to Mary Magdalene after his resurrection and told her, *"Don't cling to me... for I haven't yet ascended to the Father. But go find my brothers and tell them that I am ascending to my Father and your Father, to my God and your God."*[227] It is important to know that this meeting took place after his crucifixion. In fact, this is crucial to know because many Trinitarians claim that what Jesus said on earth about God and himself is negated by the fact he was in human form. The claim goes that as a human Jesus was only able to teach from a human perspective. Trinitarians insist, however, that his point of view would be different after his resurrection. There can be no misunderstanding Christ's meaning: he died; he was resurrected by God; and he was going to join God in heaven.

Jesus didn't say that he had become God.

He said he was going to be with God; the same God that was the center of Jesus' ministry; the same God in which his fellow Jews believed and prayed; the Almighty God found in Hebrew scripture; the supreme god known as Yahweh. Jesus was resurrected to his place of honor at the right hand of Yahweh.

5 The Spirit of...

There is a spirit within people, the breath of the Almighty within them, that makes them intelligent. Job 32:8

If it seems that I haven't devoted much time to the holy spirit it's for good reason, neither did the majority of the early Christian writers. At least, not in the way that it has been portrayed in modern churches. Today mainstream churches teach that the *Holy Spirit* (or *Holy Ghost*), is the third leg of the God Trifecta otherwise known as the Trinity. We will see that this is simply not biblical. Yes, at times God's spirit (active force or power) is spoken of metaphorically (e.g., it is personified in John[228] and likened to a dove descending from heaven during Christ's baptism[229]), but so too are many other concepts in the Bible. The Bible, like any other literary work, abounds with metaphor and allegory to describe all kinds of actions and emotions.

As an example, metaphors have been used to describe the concept of sin at various times throughout the Bible. We find in the Old Testament that: "*sin is crouching*" at one's door like a wild beast that must be subdued and mastered;[230] "*sin runs rampant;*"[231] "*sin whispers to the wicked;*"[232] and that dishonest people "*give birth to sin.*"[233] This type of metaphorical description of sin carried over into the New Testament as well. As an example, Paul personified sin in his letter to the Romans.[234] And the language that Paul used is not unlike the kind he used to explain the indwelling of God's spirit in believers. For instance, Paul described sin as living inside himself; he portrayed sin as an internal slave master who forced Paul to sin against his own will; and he claimed that sin actually used the Mosaic Law to further sin's own "*evil purposes.*" Paul even went as far as putting the entire blame on sin for the wrongs committed by Paul himself! In short, we see that the use of metaphor is clearly used to describe the abstract concept of sin. And so it is with God's reaction to sin.

We are told in Job that sinners should be made to "*drink deeply of the anger of the Almighty.*"[235] This liquid analogy to Yahweh's anger doesn't end there. There are many references to God's anger or fury being "*poured out*" on various groups for their disobedience throughout the Bible.[236] The most graphic example is from the prophet Jeremiah who was told to bring a "*cup filled to the brim*" with God's anger to various nations, which, once consumed, would make them "*stagger,*" "*drunk,*" *vomit*" and finally "*fall.*"[237] Apparently God's spirit of anger is poured out just as readily as his love, yet no one is suggesting that his anger is part of the godhead, even though identical language is used in its description. While we're on the subject, besides anger the Bible records that judgment, fate, blessings, life, grace, special favor, man's spirit, and even lust have all been "*poured out*" at one time or another.[238]

Holy libations Batman! That's a lot of pouring!

The writers of the above scriptures weren't being literal. They were using all the literary tools, including metaphors, at their disposal. And quite possibly the most powerful metaphor of all is personification because we, as humans, can relate most readily to each other. The personification of objects and thoughts is actually quite a common practice in everyday speech. Every time we use feminine pronouns when referring to cars, boats or any other inanimate object we are personifying them to rationalize our endearment to them. More importantly, human attributes applied to a thought or an idea allows one to comprehend and embrace it at a deeper level, with the added bonus of giving it poetic flair.

An excellent example of an abstraction personified in scripture can be found in the opening chapter of Proverbs, "*Come and listen to my counsel. I'll share my heart with you and make you wise… all who listen to me will live in peace, untroubled by fear of harm.*"[239] So sayeth the spirit of Chokmah in a monologue that extends for twelve verses. The spirit of *Chokmah*, (Hebrew for *wisdom*), had a strong and protracted feminine voice in the Old Testament; she spoke with wonderful vigor and candidness. The spirit of Chokmah corrected, admonished, questioned, pleaded, insulted and finally declared divine retribution on the *"simpletons"* who refused to take heed and acknowledge the advice that came from her.

The gifts that come from Chokmah are quite impressive: peace, joy, happiness, protection, longevity, and honor.[240] It is said that the spirit of Chokmah will save men from immoral women, and all of us from evil people.[241] Chokmah explained that a lavish palace with a great feast inside has been prepared for all who wish to partake, *"Come in with me… Come, eat my food, and drink the wine I have mixed. Leave your simple ways behind, and begin to live; learn to use good judgment."*[242] It is interesting to note that although Chokmah *"shouts in the streets,"*[243] there are times when Chokmah can apparently become quite difficult to find.[244] However, once we do find her we are to *"embrace"* and love *Chokmah "like a sister."*[245]

The Bible wonderfully describes the benefits of receiving the spirit of Chokmah; Yahweh gifted many *"skilled craftsmen"* with her spirit so that they would be better able to perform their tasks.[246] Joshua was known to be full of the spirit of Chokmah, *"for Moses laid his hands on him."*[247] Thus, Joshua was empowered by her spirit (via Moses) to lead the Israelites into the Promised Land. This is perhaps the first example in the Bible of a spirit being imparted from one person to another.

While it is true that Chokmah's key speaking parts are found in the Old Testament, the two main men of the New Testament also give it some kudos. Paul wonderfully described the spirit of Chokmah as the *"mystery of God"* to the church in Corinth;[248] Paul even prayed to God send her to the Ephesians so that they might better be able know God.[249] Finally, Jesus declared that Chokmah would be justified by her children.[250] Indeed, Jesus himself as a child was filled with the very spirit of Chokmah.[251] In the New Testament, however, the spirit of Chokmah would be known as Sophia, her Greek name. We learn from James that Sophia is first and foremost *"pure."* He also described her as *"peace loving, gentle at all times, and willing to yield to others."*[252] Finally, Chokmah is described as nothing less than the *"tree of life."*[253] Yahweh, in fact, founded the earth by the power of Chokmah.[254]

With all of the above scriptures at their disposal it's easy to understand why certain Gnostic sects believed Sophia was a deity in her own right. Valentinus went as far as to say that the goddess Sophia actually created all beings, including Yahweh himself.[255] The abstract concept of wisdom had been personified to the point that it was considered a deity well before the holy spirit was ever thought of as such. This isn't surprising considering that the *spirit of wisdom* has an actual speaking part in the Bible; the same can't be said about the holy spirit, or the *spirit of holiness* as it's more properly rendered.

At times the *spirit of wisdom* can be found mingling with the *spirit of holiness* in scripture. We can see two examples of their simultaneous appearances in the book of Acts. The first involved the Apostles' selection of men to be in charge of distributing food within their community. After much deliberation, the decision was made to choose well respected men who were full of both, the spirit of holiness *and* the spirit of wisdom.[256] Apparently, to the Apostles the holy spirit on its own wasn't enough, which is surprising if the holy spirit is a god. However, if the spirit of holiness is an attitude then it makes perfect sense that the Apostles would also require that this attitude be tempered with or steeped in wisdom. As a second example we turn to Stephen and his proselytization abilities; scripture recounts that there wasn't anyone who tried to debate him that *"could stand against the wisdom and the Spirit with which Stephen spoke."*[257] Once again, wisdom is recognized as an equally crucial facet, alongside the spirit.

Wisdom is cast in the same light as the holy spirit in the above examples. So if the spirit is imagined to be a god, why not wisdom? Why isn't the goddess Sophia part of the Godhead? The spirit of wisdom can and should be considered more of a deity than the spirit of holiness, that is, if we discount or downplay the use of metaphors by the various authors of the Bible. After all, the spirit of wisdom speaks, and she speaks loudly. However, if we acknowledge the use of artistic license, and take into consideration the overall context of the Bible, then we can correctly ascertain that wisdom was simply personified for the sake of poetic flair. The same can be said about the holy spirit; it was personified for the sake of poetic flair, nothing more.

Incidentally, alongside the spirits of wisdom and holiness we find an assortment of other *spirits* in the Bible, many of which are simply abstractions brought to life through the magic of metaphor. Everything from foolishness[258] to prostitution[259] to fear[260] to humility[261] has been written about as having a *spirit*. With so many varied references it becomes obvious that *the spirit* did not automatically imply a sentient being, or evoke some sort of personhood. Rather, it was commonly attached to words used to described attitudes or ideas, or to induce an emotional connection. While it's true that God's spirit has, at times, been personified, this in itself doesn't point to it being an actual deity any more than it does for wisdom, foolishness, fear, humility or prostitution. Many ideas and emotions have been immortalized, so to speak, in the pages of the Bible by the able use of metaphor. To read scripture without this simple but obvious fact leaves its reader unequipped to comprehend a large portion of the Bible; and it renders the Bible devoid of literary substance. Yet this is exactly the way it must be read in order for the Trinity to have any substance. The rules of language have to be suspended.

The writers of the Bible didn't give the holy spirit the type of recognition that the Trinity doctrine implies because it wasn't considered a god by either Jews or early Christians. Nor was it ever suggested by them that it was be worshipped in addition to and alongside Yahweh.

This, in fact, would go against everything for which Judaism stood, and against the wishes of both Yahweh and Jesus. It took well into the 4th century, the intervention of the newly converted emperor, and two church councils for the divinity of the holy spirit to get completely formulated. The first of such gatherings, which would subsequently be known as the 1st Ecumenical Council, took place in a town called Nicaea in the year 325 at the behest of Emperor Constantine who wanted to unify Christianity, and by extension, his dominion. Even as church leaders were trying to come to some consensus on the status of Jesus, the holy spirit was basically footnoted. The original creed hammered out and signed there by the majority of bishops only casually and briefly acknowledged it in its last sentence.

That was it.

It didn't acquire divine status until centuries after the time of Christ. Accordingly, the phrase holy spirit (or Holy Ghost) was never used as a proper name by the writers of the Bible. It is simply an equivalent of the phrases *spirit of God* and *spirit of Yahweh*, both of which are used throughout Jewish and Christian scripture to describe God's active force or influence.[262] The two root Greek words involved are *hagios* and *pneuma*. *Hagios* simply means *holy* or *sacred*, while *pneuma* is much more diverse. It is used to denote everything from air, wind, and breathing, to spiritual entities and attitudes. Unfortunately, based on modern usage it's easy to assume that it is a proper name for a few reasons. To begin with, the first letter of each word is always capitalized, which in the English language signifies a proper name. That they are capitalized would make perfect sense if the earliest manuscripts weren't written using majuscule script, writing that consisted of all capital letters; lowercase letters didn't exist. So the decision to treat the phrase as a proper name (and capitalize the first letter of each word) was made by translators long after the first texts were written.

Moreover, the phrase *holy spirit* as it stands isn't found nearly as often in the original texts as it is in modern translations. Nonetheless, in a concerted effort to give it a more prominent role in scripture, the holy spirit has been shoehorned into modern texts wherever it is deemed even remotely plausible. As a result, you're as likely to find the phrase *spirit of holiness* (with and without the definite article *the* (Greek: *ho* or *to*) as you are *holy spirit* in the original manuscripts, yet they're treated as identical by translators.

This is very misleading in and of itself because similar redacting doesn't occur regarding the phrases *spirit of Yahweh* and *spirit of God*, both of which are found dozens of times in the Bible. We don't find either translated as *Yahweh's spirit* or *God's spirit* because it would undermine the idea of the holy spirit's personhood by allowing a comparison between the three. The phrases *spirit of holiness*, *spirit of Yahweh* and *spirit of God* are equivalent in meaning. Yet they're not treated as such in modern translations.

To make matters worse, if you compare modern translations to early Greek manuscripts you'll find that the former have deliberately redacted scriptures to include the phrase without having the textual support to do so. As an example, the NLT translated *"to pneuma tes aletheias"* (the spirit of truth) found in John 14:17 and 15:26 as *"the Holy Spirit."* You will also find many occasions where *spirit* has been unjustly retrofitted with the word *holy*, again, simply to give *the holy spirit* a greater presence in scripture. So, for instance, when Jesus compares the concepts of the flesh and the spirit in a conversation with Nicodemus, the editors of the NLT have inserted *holy* into the scripture even though the Greek texts clearly have the word *spirit* by itself.[263] Finally, modern Bibles have translated the Greek word *auto* as the pronoun *he* whenever it's connected to the word *spirit* (pneuma) even though it can be as readily translated as *it*. The implications are obvious.

In sum, a variety of misleading translating techniques have been used to bolster the image of the holy spirit as a deity. Individually these translating errors are problematic; collectively they sabotage the efforts of the original authors of the Bible who espouse the importance of worshipping Yahweh alone. Remove the translating bias that is present in most modern translations and the true nature of the holy spirit becomes obvious; it is God's power and influence over a believer; it is Yahweh's active force influencing his creations. This force can be understood in both natural and supernatural terms. It can influence a person's attitude naturally, as a byproduct of accepting God and embracing all that Christianity entails. In this sense it is very much like the way an enthusiastic sports fan can be said to have team spirit; or the way a member of the armed services can eat, drink and sleep with the military mindset. Peter and Paul both wrote to Christians about the importance of having "*one mind,*" with one thought and purpose.[264]

Conversely, an individual can also receive Yahweh's spirit supernaturally, either directly from Yahweh himself, as when Jesus received the spirit in the form of a dove during his baptism;[265] or indirectly, as in the laying of hands by men already infused with the power of God. We get an excellent example of this indirect approach in the book of Acts. The Apostles Peter and John were doing just this (laying hands on believers and imparting God's spirit) when a sorcerer named Simon asked if he could purchase the capacity to channel God's power for himself. Simon, of course, was rebuked for his insolence, but the episode exemplifies the essence of the spirit of holiness.[266] It can described as Yahweh's power channeled through an individual. The spirit of holiness in this sense has empowered persons to accomplish extraordinary feats both large and small; from receiving the gift of prophecy,[267] to the ability to perform miracles[268] and raise the dead;[269] to just feeling God's presence in some slight but poignant way. The holy spirit is simply the pure and sacred influence of the Almighty; an influence that, if accepted, can positively impact and empower the beneficiary.

More often than not, this holy power is spoken of in objective, elemental terms. As an example, New Testament writers used the same terminology to describe his spirit of holiness as they did for his spirit of anger; they routinely used liquid metaphors. This, in fact, can be seen throughout the Bible. The prophet Isaiah, for instance, predicated that one day God's spirit would be *"poured out… from heaven;"*[270] Micah, another Old Testament prophet, proclaimed that he was *"filled with power—with the Spirit of [Yahweh];"*[271] we learn from Peter at the home of the gentile Cornelius that *"the gift of the Holy Spirit had been poured out on the Gentiles;"*[272] and Paul wrote to Titus that the spirit of holiness, which God "*poured through Jesus,*" "*washed away our sins.*"[273] Perhaps Paul made the most apt correlation of them all when he contrasted the negative results of being filled with wine to being *"filled with the Holy Spirit."*[274] Further, he said that Jews and gentiles alike *"have all been made to drink into one Spirit."*[275]

The spirit is also consistently likened to wind or air throughout the Bible, as in Genesis when Yahweh "*breathed the breath of life*" into man.[276] Correspondingly, the resurrected Jesus imparted the spirit to his disciples by breathing on them.[277] As another example, Peter pointed out in Jerusalem that gentile believers had received the spirit in the same fashion as he and the other disciples had previously received it; God's spirit came with *"the roaring of a mighty windstorm, and it filled the house where they were sitting."*[278]

Examples abound in scripture of the spirit being metaphorically poured out or filling up a believer. It's difficult to imagine that they are referring to an individual deity who will reside in each and every believer in God, when such obvious objective language is used. However, it makes perfect sense to describe God's *power* as filling up, being poured out upon, or breathed into the lucky recipients. We find an incident in the Bible that best exemplifies God's spirit or power in action, in which Jesus felt this very power involuntarily leave him. Without his prior knowledge or consent a woman had been healed by simply touching his robe. In this instance Jesus was merely the conduit of God's power; by Christ's own words the woman's faith was the catalyst for her healing.[279]

So how did the holy spirit come to be known as a god in its own right?

The culmination of the evolution of the *"Spirit of Yahweh"* from his force or power into an actual separate being can be traced directly to the 2nd Ecumenical Council in the year 381. There it was formally decided that this third leg of the Trinity would forevermore be considered a living god alongside Yahweh and Jesus. It took three and a half centuries and a lot of human effort but the holy spirit finally made it to the big time to become the third of three gods recognized as part of the so-called Godhead. It even has the capital letters to prove it. It's just too bad that it's not true.

To be sure, this spirit is not to be taken lightly or belittled; that is not my intention. The spirit is the power of God and deserves to be properly respected. After all, Jesus pointed out that the ultimate blasphemy is against the spirit, which is the only sin that would not be forgiven.[280] He, in fact, even placed the spirit over himself: *"Anyone who speaks against the Son of Man can be forgiven, but anyone who speaks against the Holy Spirit will never be forgiven, either in this world or in the world to come."*[281] Those were strong words; and hard to misunderstand. Simply put, we are never to denounce or deny the power of Yahweh when we see or feel it in action.

6 Trinity

> *You are following a different way that pretends to be the Good News but is not the Good News at all. You are being fooled by those who deliberately twist the truth concerning Christ.* Galatians 1:6-7

It is interesting to me that oft times whenever the validity of the Trinity is questioned proponents of it quickly concede that the word is not found in the Bible; neither are Godhead, Triune or any other words that can remotely be interpreted to represent the Trinity. To me this is a pretty good hint the concept didn't exist among early Christians; to them it's a wondrous mystery. To me when the prophets of the Old Testament, the Apostles of the New Testament, and Jesus Christ himself, all spoke of believing in one God, I say okay; Trinitarians will say, *"Yes! One God! One - like a cluster of grapes!"*[282]

A cluster of grapes.

This example very clearly highlights the strange habit that permeates the world of religion, which is the proclivity of finding more meaning in the written word than what was originally intended. I am not referring to the typical literary tools such as metaphors, and similes that we discussed in the prior chapter. I'm talking about the deliberate creation of new, mystical definitions of typical words in an effort to justify manmade doctrine. To prove their theories, believers in the Trinity (and the Oneness doctrine) are zealously reinventing definitions of otherwise ordinary words found in the Bible, to better accommodate their beliefs. Words such as *one*, for instance. It is simply impossible for the Trinity to exist and *one* to actually mean *one* in this, and many other scriptures. So this otherwise innocuous word is reinvented.

Eric Hoffer rightly observed:

> When some part of a doctrine is relatively simple, there is a tendency among the faithful to complicate and obscure it. Simple words are made pregnant with meaning and made to look like symbols in a secret message.[283]

The problem is that Dan Brown didn't write the Bible; and you shouldn't need an English to Christian interlinear dictionary to grasp its overarching theme. Nor should you need a translator in the form of the clergy. The Old Testament is rife with proclamations from Yahweh himself that he is the one and only supreme God who is to be worshipped exclusively. He is very clear about this, as were his prophets. Furthermore, this message was reinforced by Jesus and his disciples in the New Testament. Yet Trinitarians maintain that, amidst these assertions, the doctrine of the Godhead was lying dormant just waiting to be unveiled by energetic go-getters. Their conclusions, however, fail to take into consideration the context and the basic grammar and syntax of the scriptures to which they refer. They have faith in the Trinity doctrine, so whatever needs to be adjusted in order to make it jibe is adjusted. Nevertheless, tweaking the scriptures and saying *it's a mystery* doesn't make it true.

To believers in the doctrine, the mere mention of Yahweh, Jesus and the spirit in the same breath is affirmation of some holy triptych of equality that they share together. However, with the exception of a single scripture this type of relationship between them is not mentioned in the Bible. Besides the above, I've probably mentioned the three in the same sentence on numerous occasions in this book. I do not believe in their equality or the Trinity in any way shape of form, yet by using their logic this entire book has now become proof of the existence of the Trinity!

Belief in the Trinity doctrine presupposes a bridge that transitions the concept of the single, supreme God (Yahweh) explicitly mentioned in the Bible, to the implied concept of three separate but equal gods that form the Godhead. It is implied because there aren't any scriptures that explicitly describe the Godhead save one: 1st John 5:7, which, we will see, is of dubious origin. It is also implied because Jesus never asked to be worshipped; neither did the holy spirit. Therefore in order for this tritheistic bridge to be sound, it must be built upon a foundation of scripture that, through sheer supposition, substantiates five key points which are necessary for the doctrine to be true:

1) Jesus was an eternal being that came down to earth;[284]
2) The holy spirit is an actual being and not simply Yahweh's power;
3) The holy spirit is a God;
4) Jesus and the holy spirit are both equal to Yahweh;
5) Jesus and the holy spirit are both to be worshipped alongside Yahweh.

The truth of the Trinity is completely and wholly dependent upon the veracity of these five points, all of which must also be reconciled with the existence of the single God explicitly supported by the Bible. For centuries these points have been accepted as fact, propagated primarily by the Roman Catholic Church, and continued with Protestantism after the Reformation; scriptural support, however, simply does not exist. This is why it took well into the 4th century (and much heated debate) for its final form to emerge.[285] It took that long to fabricate a believable explanation from a hodgepodge of scriptural snippets. Of course, it didn't hurt that the majority of civilization was illiterate and no longer spoke Latin, the preferred language of the Church. After all, who would have been able to challenge the clergy as to the content or meaning of scripture if no one could read or speak Latin? The Church stayed with Latin for this very reason. And that's why for centuries church leaders fought tooth and nail against any and every one who tried to translate the Bible into other languages, enacting laws which were punishable by death for the offense. Eventually, though, men did translate the Bible into other languages, and in the process, uncovered some very interesting discrepancies. As we will see, included in these discrepancies is the above mentioned scripture found in 1st John.

The eminent textual critic Professor Bart Ehrman rightly pointed out in his book *Misquoting Jesus* that the only scripture in the entire Bible that can be said to overtly represent the Trinity is found in 1st John.[286] It reads: *"For there are three that bear witness in heaven: the Father, the Word, and the Holy Spirit; and these three are one."*[287] Now, for such an important church doctrine one would think that Jesus and all of his disciples would have had at least a few more comments attributed to them that were similar in context. It should also go without saying that some reference to the Godhead should have been made by an Old Testament prophet or two, or even by Yahweh himself. He had no problem making himself abundantly clear to his people about many other issues, such as the need to provide for widows and orphans. This is explicitly discussed throughout the Bible. So why not do the same with such a vital and fundamental piece of Christian theology? Especially since it refutes the most obvious and basic message in the Old Testament, which is the absolute demand for Yahweh to be worshipped exclusively?

Well, at least they have 1st John 5:7 and one is better than none. Except that there seems to be a problem with the validity of the scripture. So much so that many Bibles mention the discrepancy in their footnotes. In fact, along with its explanation the NLT relegates a substantial portion of the questionable scripture to a footnote. The amended verse seven, combined with eight reads:

> *"So we have these three witnesses* - the Spirit, the water, and the blood - and all three agree."*

NLT's footnote includes the statement:

> "A few very late manuscripts add *in heaven—the Father, the Word, and the Holy Spirit, and these three are one. And we have three witnesses on earth."*

Traditionally the phrase in question would be inserted at the asterisk. Why would they chose to remove it in the first place? The key is in the phrase *"a few very late manuscripts,"* which forces us to step back in time to the early 1500's to meet the Dutch textual scholar Desiderius Erasmus. Erasmus is credited with having produced the first published edition of the New Testament (in Greek), working from Greek manuscripts dated from between the 10th and 13th centuries. Although he worked primarily from two, rather mediocre 12th century manuscripts, his Greek-Latin parallel New Testament was a giant improvement from what had been available at that time. In the course of translating Erasmus had come to realize that the Roman Catholic's primary version of the Bible was full of errors. With his translation Erasmus aimed to correct what he considered the badly corrupted text of the *Latin Vulgate*.

Among his many amendments was the removal of the phrase in question. None of the Greek manuscripts at his disposal had the phrase, so he left it out of his first and second editions. When questioned by some church leaders as to the cause of the omission Erasmus had told them as much. Apparently Erasmus was told that he couldn't remove the scripture, as their doctrine of the Trinity hinged upon it. Erasmus replied by promising that if they could produce a Greek manuscript which included the scripture then he would put it in a subsequent edition.

Well, *produce* one they did.

Being a man of his word Erasmus included it in his next edition, which was to become the primary New Testament source for the vast majority, if not all, subsequent translations for centuries to come, including the 1611 edition of the King James Bible.

Fast forward to the 21st century.

Hundreds of early Greek manuscripts that predate those used by Erasmus have since been discovered in the ensuing years. None of them include the phrase in question. Virtually all biblical scholars agree that the manuscript handed to Erasmus was probably created during his time, with the scripture in question reverse translated from the Latin Vulgate. The phrase simply did not come from the same hand that penned the letter; the vast majority of scholars agree that the scripture was a later addition. Therefore, with the exception of 1st John 5:7, which was inserted into the letter long after it was originally penned, there isn't a single sentence in the entire Bible that explicitly describes the Trinity doctrine. It had to be cajoled out of the Bible by men reading between the lines and making inferences as to the *true* meaning of the texts. This true meaning only revealed itself after the words of the texts themselves were redefined to support their interpretation.

This brings up a serious question: if the Trinity is firmly rooted in the writings of 1st century Christians why would the church need to fabricate evidence? This in and of itself lends credibility to the notion that early evidence for the Trinity is, in fact, sorely lacking. So where, or more precisely, when did the Trinity originate?

The origin of doctrine…

They traded the truth about God for a lie. So they worshiped and served the things God created instead of the Creator himself, who is worthy of eternal praise! Roman 1:25

For all practical considerations, the Trinity is a byproduct of the dual misconceptions of gentile believers that the earthly Jesus was a god in human form (incarnate), and that, like his heavenly Father, he had no beginning (he is eternal). Putting aside for the moment that Jesus never claimed to be either eternal or a god incarnate, these two beliefs would prove to be at odds with traditional Judaism's teaching of a single, supreme God put forth in Jewish scripture, and with Christ's message. Former pagans wrestling with this dilemma (reconciling their newfound belief in Jesus with the monotheistic view of Judaism) would naturally gravitate towards a system with which they would be familiar. And so the Trinity doctrine was concocted to try and merge the misconceptions about Jesus with Judaism to form a cohesive theological system that would stand up to scrutiny. The triadic concept of gods had been extremely popular in pagan religions; nearly all cultures had some form of it. In his essay, *A Psychological Approach to the Dogma of the Trinity,* Carl Jung points out that religious triads have existed since the earliest civilizations. For instance, ancient Babylon had the triadic group of Anu, Bel and Ea; Egypt had Osiris, Isis and Horus; while the classical Greek triad consisted of Zeus, Athena, and Apollo. Christianity would soon follow suit with a triadic formula of its own in an attempt to reconcile three gods within the traditional monotheistic framework of Judaism.

Ironically, Jesus never asked to be worshiped. Yet in their zeal the recently converted enthusiastically tried to understand the role of Jesus through their existing religious construct. And, thanks to Hellenistic influences, this construct included the concept of gods in human form. Greek and Roman mythology are rife with stories of gods that came down to earth to dwell with man. So, even though he himself never said as much, it seemed plausible to these new believers that Jesus was just another one of these gods. What they failed to take into consideration was that this, in fact, contradicted the basic tenets of the theology that Jesus advocated.

Furthermore, many of the early Christian apologists were trained in the Greek philosophic schools prior to becoming Christian. When they converted to Christianity they brought their prior education with them, applying it to their new religion. An excellent example of the influence of Greek culture upon Christians can be found in the New Testament itself. Paul's letter to the Romans was to serve as a formal introduction for Paul and his theology to the church in Rome. Although he was Jewish we can see from this letter that he had been educated in the Greek style of rational thought and argumentation, which he used throughout his letter. Paul's extensive use of imaginary speakers to create a dialogue, his use of rhetorical questions, his personification of thought or ideas, and his use of hypothetical objections to his arguments that he summarily refutes are all literary features of the classical Greek diatribe.

This Hellenistic influence on Christianity continued until by the 4th century Christian theologians, such as Gregory of Nazianzus, had gone beyond trying to explain how it was possible to believe in three gods and still be a monotheist. He, along with brothers Basil, Bishop of Caesarea and Gregory, Bishop of Nyssa (collectively known as the Cappadocian Fathers), assured all those who would listen that there could be no other possibility because, after all, God is the greatest mystery there is and the paradox of the Trinity proved it.[288] Thus, as far as Cappadocians were concerned, the enigma of the Trinity had been created as an explanation to the inexplicable; the explanation is there isn't one. The result of this sophism is the Christianity we have today; not the Christianity that the first Christians espoused.

Let's back up a little and examine both issues (the incarnation and the eternality of Jesus) more closely.

It's easy enough to understand how the notion of Jesus being a god on earth could have originated. Jesus lived amidst pagan cultures which were full of gods that came down to earth and slept with humans to create divine heroes. And while the legend of Heracles is an excellent pagan example of this, we only have to look in Genesis to see the same concept in action immortalized in scripture. A group of spiritual beings known as the *"sons of God"* came down to earth to bed the *"daughters of men."* These unholy unions created a race of giant *"mighty men"* known as Nephilites who in ancient times became *"men of renown."*[289] This story, in fact, could be an archaic reference to demigods of Greek mythology. In any case, it would be quite easy to assume Jesus fit into this category of demigod, especially if the story of his divine birth and resurrection is taken into consideration. Alexander the Great was considered just this type of person. The belief that he was the son of Zeus is documented in ancient writings.

Besides the possibility of being an offspring of a god, there are other occasions when divinity was posthumously bestowed upon historical persons of great prominence. Plato, for instance, was considered a son of the god Apollo by later generations. And starting with the Blessed Virgin Mary, just try to count all of the Catholic saints that were posthumously declared divine and you'll get an idea of how easy it is for believers to accept the sanctity of another human being.[290] Finally, the ancient world abounded with mythological stories of gods that visited earth for a time in human form. This explains how the citizens of Lystra easily mistook Paul and Barnabas for the Greek Gods Hermes and Zeus.[291] Legend had it that this type of visitation in Lystra had occurred in the past.[292]

It is comprehensible that some would hear of the miracles performed by Jesus (and of his resurrection) and wrongly conclude that he had been a god on earth. The same can be seen in the actions of untold Muslims and Buddhists who exalt and worship the two founders of their faiths as divine even though Muhammad and Buddha both insisted that they were merely human. What might not have been heard as loudly or as readily believed was that Jesus attributed everything-all of his power-to the Jewish god Yahweh. Jesus also maintained that his followers would be able to do the same and more, which, as the Bible illustrates, happened.[293] His disciples performed miracles, healed the sick, and even raised the dead, just like Jesus promised.[294]

Finally, one major point overlooked completely is that Jesus didn't raise himself from the dead. Christ's final words on the cross are quite telling: *"Father, I entrust my spirit into your hands!"*[295] Without his Father's mercy, Jesus would have never been resurrected. The message of the resurrection is not that Jesus overcame the grave by his own volition; it is that Yahweh plucked Jesus from death and that he would do the same for us, *if* we have faith.[296] Jesus is only one of nine individuals recorded in the Bible that were raised from the dead through the power of Yahweh. This number doesn't include all those that were said to come back to life en masse upon Christ's death. [297]

The gospel of John is the only book in the Bible that can be said to infer the status of divinity upon Jesus. This was a new and strikingly different position; one that stood apart from earlier biblical writings; and one of the many significant ways that John's gospel differed from the other three. John's confusion makes perfect sense because by the time of its writing (six or seven decades after the death of Jesus), and for the reasons outlined above, the idea had begun to be kicked around that Jesus had been a god on earth. However, there is one thing that's absolutely certain: according to the Bible **Jesus never claimed to be a god**.

This includes the gospel of John.

Contrary to Trinitarian's misappropriation of scripture, he also never implied it. As we've learned, every single scripture that has been used to suggest that Jesus inferred he was a god has been excised from their original context to do so. And yes, this includes the gospel of John.

The second key issue which needed clarification is the question of Christ's origin. Is he a created being, or is he eternal? This would turn out to be a stickier topic because his coequality depends entirely upon it. There is no way around the fact that Jesus needs to be eternal in order to be his Father's equal. Accordingly, this second issue was eventually debated more rigorously than the issue of his earthly divinity. I must reiterate that, according to the Bible, Jesus never claimed to be eternal. Yet, once again, what Jesus said was irrelevant to those that disagreed with him.

The dispute reached a full head of steam in the 4th century when leaders of the church, gathering in the town of Nicaea (present day Iznik Turkey), would take a formal stance as to the origin and nature of Jesus. This stance, known today as the Nicene Creed, officially professed that Jesus was of the same essence, or substance, of his heavenly Father. The Council of Nicaea also reinterpreted the word *begotten* to preclude the traditional definition of *made,* or *created*, in an attempt to circumvent the discontinuity between their belief and scripture. They rationalized that removing these definitions would solve the problem of Christ's eternality refuting scripture. However, as we shall see their new interpretation of *begotten* completely contradicted the traditional definition used throughout scripture; it also ran contrary to the majority of early church fathers who acknowledged in their writings that Jesus had undeniably been created.

Let's start with Polycarp.

Believed to be a student of none other than the Apostle John himself, Polycarp's death in 155 is recorded in a letter written by his congregation in Smyrna where he had been bishop. *The Martyrdom of Polycarp* recounts his final hours on earth before he was burned at the stake. The letter acknowledged Polycarp's admirable skill as a teacher and martyr. It then closed by giving thanks and praise to God for access into his eternal kingdom. This access is gained only by the believing in God's "only-begotten Son."[298] From this letter we can ascertain that Polycarp taught his congregation that God created Jesus.

Writing about the same time was a philosopher turned Christian who, after his death in 166, would come to be known as Justin the Martyr. Among his body of work we can find evidence that he also understood that Jesus had a beginning. In his work *First Apology* Justin contrasted "the only unbegotten God" to his son Jesus, who was "born of God in a peculiar manner, different from ordinary generation..."[299] He reiterated these same thoughts in his *Second Apology*, once again declaring God the Father to be unbegotten, while acknowledging that Jesus "was begotten before the world."[300]

Next we move to Tatian, a student of Justin and probable author of the Diatessaron, which is an amalgamation of Matthew, Mark, Luke and John. His goal in doing so was to create a unified gospel free of the discrepancies that exist among the four. This was the gospel of choice in Syrian churches until the 4th century when they began using the four individual ones. In addition to the Diatessaron, Tatian also wrote an apology entitled *Tatian's Address to the Greeks*, in which he asserted that God was at one time totally alone until he created his "first-begotten work," Jesus Christ.[301]

Then there is Irenaeus, one of the most influential church fathers of his time. Irenaeus began his Christian life in the town of Smyrna as a student of Polycarp, before moving to Gaul (modern day France) where he eventually became Bishop of Lyons until his death in 202 or 3. Most known for his ongoing campaign against Gnosticism, his five volume work, *Against Heresies,* has been invaluable for historians trying to piece together the various early forms of Christianity that had shared the spotlight with what would become Orthodox Christianity. Prior to the discovery of the Gnostic texts at Nag Hammadi in the 1940's, *Against Heresies* had been a major source of information regarding these early Christian beliefs, primarily because any text that disagreed with the Orthodox Church was considered heretical and summarily destroyed. However, based on the arguments of Irenaeus against these other sects, historians have reconstructed the majority of these unorthodox strands. The texts at Nag Hammadi merely confirmed what had been suspected thanks to *Heresies.*

Irenaeus is the go-to guy among the early church fathers when it comes to distinguishing heretical ideas from the true teachings of the first Christians. If Jesus was thought of as eternal by Irenaeus and other early Christians, Irenaeus would have defended it to the bitter end. What we find, in fact, is the exact opposite. His list of heretics in *Against Heresies* included those that denied "the salvation of him who was first created."[302] More specifically, Irenaeus denounced several men who had taught differing ideas pertaining to the origin of Jesus:

> If any one, therefore, says to us, "How then was the Son produced by the Father?" we reply to him, that no man understands that production, or generation, or calling, or revelation, or by whatever name one may describe His generation, which is in fact altogether indescribable. Neither Valentinus, nor Marcion, nor Saturninus, nor Basilides, nor angels, nor archangels, nor principalities, nor powers [possess this knowledge], but the Father only who begat, and the Son who was begotten.
> *Against Heresies,* Book 2, Chap. 28, vs. 6.[303]

As far as Irenaeus was concerned, no one knew how it happened, just that it happened. Jesus the son was begotten by Yahweh the Father. In other words, Jesus had a beginning; he was not eternal. This was the collective mindset of the vast majority of early Christians. We can see from the writings of Theophilus of Antioch (d. 181), Athenagoras (d. 190), Clement of Alexandria (d. about 220), Tertullian (d. 230), Hippolytus (d. 235), Novatian (d. 258) and Lactantius (d. 330) that Jesus had been created by the uncreated God.

The last of the church fathers that we will visit was recognized by his peers and successors as one of the most productive writers in the early church's history. Origin (d. 253), who trained under Clement of Alexander, distinguished himself at an early age as a gifted student. At the young age of eighteen Origin was chosen by Bishop Demetrius to succeed Clement as head of the Christian school of Alexandria. Among Origin's many works is his *Commentary on John's Gospel*, in which he methodically analyzed the gospel right down to grammar and syntax. The second of this ambitious ten book dissertation begins by an examination of the opening line of the gospel. Origin gave a very detailed explanation of John's use of the word god (Greek: *theos*) in relation to "the God… the uncreated cause of all things," and "the first-born of all creation, who is the first to be with God, and… is a being of more exalted rank than the other gods beside Him, of whom God is the God."[304] To put it plainly, Origin agreed with the writer of John who saw the distinction between Yahweh, the uncreated supreme God, and Jesus, the firstborn of God.

The leading church fathers of the first three centuries all agreed that Jesus was created. Or, to use a popular medieval term, he was *begotten*. This, in fact, is the term used by the New King James Bible several times:

> *And the Word became flesh and dwelt among us, and we beheld His glory, the glory as of the only* ***begotten*** *of the Father, full of grace and truth.*
>
> John 1:14 NKJV (Emphasis added.)

> *For God so loved the world that He gave His only* ***begotten*** *Son, that whoever believes in Him should not perish but have everlasting life.*
>
> John 3:16 NKJV (Emphasis added.)

> *He who believes in Him is not condemned; but he who does not believe is condemned already, because he has not believed in the name of the only* ***begotten*** *Son of God.*
>
> John 3:18 NKJV (Emphasis added.)

> *In this the love of God was manifested toward us, that God has sent His only* ***begotten*** *Son into the world, that we might live through Him.*
>
> 1st John 4:9 NKJV (Emphasis added.)

The NLT translates the Greek word *monogenes* in the above scriptures as *"one and only Son,"* which takes the teeth out of it. The word *monogenes* broken into its two root parts translates to *only-born* or *only-generated.* It's from the latter part where we get words such as gene, regenerate, generation and genesis. In other scriptures the

Greek word *prototokos* is used to describe Jesus as the *firstborn* of all creation, and the *firstborn* from the dead, who marks the beginning of the new covenant made between Yahweh and his church:

> *He is the image of the invisible God, the firstborn over all creation. For by Him all things were created that are in heaven and that are on earth... All things were created through Him and for Him. And He is before all things... And He is the head of the body, the church, who is the beginning, the firstborn from the dead, that in all things He may have the preeminence.*
>
> Colossians 1:15-18 NKJV[305]

The confusion about his prior existence comes from certain scriptures, such as Hebrews 1:2 and Genesis 1:26, which make references to Jesus being with his Father at the time of creation. While the Bible does say that Jesus was with his Father prior to the earth's existence it doesn't mean that he wasn't also created; it just means that Jesus was created first. This is in direct alignment with the teachings of Jesus himself because he never once claimed to be eternal. To the contrary, he actually admitted that he was the *"the Beginning of the creation of God."*[306] This is also in complete agreement with the vast majority of the early church leaders who acknowledged in their writings that Jesus had been created.

Hearkening back to the last chapter, some Trinitarians (and Bible translations) have reinterpreted the Greek words, *monogenes* and *prototokos,* so they don't conflict with their point of view. Rather than accepting the words at face value, their original definitions have been set aside, to be replaced by ones that conform to their doctrine. We are told by Trinitarians that when the writers of the Bible used the words *monogenes* and *prototokos* in relation to Jesus, instead of *only-generated* and *firstborn* of God, they actually meant *first in line for God's inheritance* or *sole inheritor of the Kingdom*; thus, successfully sidestepping the truth. These expanded definitions have no basis on fact. They aren't used by anyone except Christian apologetics whose sole purpose is to defend their doctrine. This includes creating fanciful interpretations for glaring contradictions between scripture and their doctrine. Not only do these definitions have no scriptural support, they completely disregard all of the other times these words are used in the Bible.

For instance, in three of the four other times we find the word *monogenes* used in the Bible it describes an only child of a mother or father.[307] The fourth concerns Abraham's son Isaac, who, while not his only child, was the only child that God counted. Isaac was the only child conceived as a result of the promise that Yahweh made with Abraham. Thus Isaac is the *only-born* or *sole child* of that promise. In other words, Isaac was the only son connected to the promise to Abraham.[308] In this respect, Ishmael, the first child born to Abraham, was completely irrelevant. Ishmael and his mother Hagar was, in fact, sent away after Isaac was born to ensure that there wouldn't be anyone to contest Isaac's position. Finally, Isaac's position as sole child was affirmed by Yahweh himself when he said that Isaac was Abraham's "*only son*."[309] Likewise, besides referring to Jesus, p*rototokos* is used in the New Testament to describe the protection that the firstborn of the Israelites received during the first

Passover,[310] and in a warning about succumbing to immorality in the manner of *"Esau, who traded his birthright as the firstborn son for a single meal."*[311]

We see through these other biblical uses that the words in question refer to created beings. These are great examples of scripture reinforcing scripture. In contrast, there isn't a single instance of either *monogenes* or *prototokos* being used in the Bible which support the creative definitions of Trinitarians. None.

The beginning of the end…

> *I know that false teachers, like vicious wolves, will come in among you after I leave, not sparing the flock. Even some men from your own group will rise up and distort the truth in order to draw a following.*
>
> Acts 20:29-30

There's a great reason it took well into the 4th century for the Orthodox Church to come to a consensus on the Trinity. There wasn't anything in the early Christian texts on which to base it. The Trinity was a doctrine that had to first be massaged into existence by its various advocates. Its major tenets then had to be nurtured through rigorous debate, starting with the divinity of Jesus in 325 at Nyssa; then continuing on with the acceptance of the spirit as a deity in 381 at Constantinople; until after much time and many disagreements the Trinity as it stands today was formally accepted by the Church. Prior to these two decisive proceedings both issues were vigorously contested with neither one being accepted as fact by the majority of the early church leaders. The debate culminated with the rise of Arianism in the first part of the 4th century

Arianism gets its name from Arius, a charismatic Alexandrian presbyter who rightly taught, as did his predecessors, that unlike his Father Jesus was not coeternal. He preached that Jesus had been created and that he was posthumously bestowed divinity by God for a job well done while on earth. Arius believed it would have defeated the purpose of Christ's visit if he been a god on earth; redemption came from the fact that Jesus was all human. Arius, incidentally, had a large and loyal following.

For those in favor of Christ's coeternity with God (and his earthly divinity), the day was won in Nyssa by a man named Athanasius whose opinion was in the minority, but who had the ear of Constantine, the Roman Emperor who had recently made Christianity the official state religion. Constantine cared more about unifying his empire than anything else and planned to use Christianity as a tool to that end. Accordingly, first and foremost Christianity needed to be unified. The determinations of the synod mattered little to Constantine. However, when he called for a meeting of the minds at Nyssa everyone else involved knew that, before they were through, the issue of Christ's prior existence had to be resolved. Athanasius felt that in order to be the savior of the world Jesus had to have coexisted with God throughout eternity, and had to have been a god on earth. A created being just couldn't cut it. So Athanasius decided that Jesus must have been of the same substance as God.

Did I mention that Athanasius was a friend of Constantine?

Take a guess how the synod turned out.

Athanasius successfully lobbied for the acceptance of what would become the Nicene Creed. This was not the end of the debate, however, because his view was in the minority. In the book, *A History of God*, distinguished author Karen Armstrong devoted an entire chapter to the evolution of the Trinity that is both thorough and engaging. She recounted that the dispute continued for at least another sixty years. Athanasius himself was sent into exile at least five times as he went in and out of favor with the powers that be.[312] It should also be noted that as bishop of Alexandria Athanasius did everything he could to restrict any and all theological speculation that disagreed with his perspective by declaring that only certain books were approved for study; books that he decided were to be included in a closed canon that survives to this day as our New Testament. By limiting theological discussions and studies to his list of approved writings Athanasius hoped to quell all dissenting opinions and direct all Christian endeavors towards his line of thought. It had its desired effect.[313]

Eventually, the ideas of Christ's coeternity with God and his divinity while on earth won out, and remain basic tenets of mainstream churches to this day. As for the holy spirit, its substance wasn't fully determined until the 2nd Ecumenical Council of 381 when it was decided that it was a full-fledged deity in its own right; a deity that deserved equal billing right alongside Jesus and Yahweh on the big screen of Christianity. We've been stuck with the Trinity ever since.

It is what it is.

The Son radiates God's own glory and expresses the very character of God...
Hebrews 1:3

Nowadays theologians have simply assumed that the Trinity is factual. [314] Consequently, rather than bothering to validate the Trinity the bulk of their myopic efforts have been aimed at explaining new and inventive ways to show that it is absolutely required. Once this "need" was established scripture was revisited and simply viewed through the lens that was fashioned with the need. By creating an indispensable need for the Trinity proponents of the doctrine have sidestepped the issue of whether or not it is valid in the first place. In a simple act of theological misdirection the problem is avoided. This type of skewed perception by Trinitarians is not unlike the Darwinistic perspective of geological evidence. Rather than objectively viewing the evidence to see whether it either informs or refutes the theory, anything that contradicts Darwinism is simply dismissed as inaccurate because their conviction in the theory itself presupposes it to be true. In their minds, it stands to reason that all evidence must either point to evolution via Darwinism or be inaccurate; it could never actually be used to prove the fallibility of a theory that is, in fact, fact. [315] In both of the above instances the cart has been placed soundly before the horse by their supporters. The doctrines of the Trinity and Darwinism are used by their devotees to interpret evidence rather than letting the evidence weigh in on the doctrines.

One such "need" that Trinitarians have favored is the presupposition that God's love necessitates the Trinity doctrine. The argument goes like this: God is love; love is relational; thus an eternal recipient of God's love must have existed. The Trinity is then used to fill this requirement. It's a sweet albeit misguided notion. This particular line of reason has, in fact, been favored as a proof for the existence of the Trinity since the Trinity's acceptation in the late 4th century, and would be all well and good if it weren't for the several glaring spurious and simplistic assertions that surround the argument.

The first issue that jumps out is that God's love is conditional, in that it needs a recipient to exist. This is viewing God's love from a very humanistic perspective, which creates unnecessary contingencies upon it and him. To put it another way, if God's love for us is relational in form, than then by proxy we control it; it is contingent upon us accepting it. If we refuse to acknowledge it then it doesn't exist. While the love of mankind can said to be relational the same cannot be automatically assumed for the creator of the universe. Actually, it is this incorrect assumption-that God's love is relational-that has lent any validity to the argument in the first place. Rather than relational (with a recipient being naturally implicit and, thus, necessary) the essence of God's love should instead be thought of as radiating.

An excellent, though very simplistic, comparison would be to the sun on a bright summer day; its energy, which emanates in all directions in the form of electromagnetic waves, still exists regardless of whether or not we are outside to bask in its warmth. The same can be said about Yahweh's love; we could either acknowledge the consummating power of his love or deny it; we are engulfed in it nonetheless.

Furthermore, whatever else the sun may be (hydrogen and helium), or the complex effects it has on the earth (both good and bad), the most important feature for us is the warming effect it has on earth which allows life to flourish. Without it life as we know it could not exist. So it can be said that, to us, the sun *is* life. In the same respect, whatever else can be ascribed to Yahweh in the way of attributes, or about the way in which he has affected the earth and mankind, for many believers God *is* love.

Finally, this is what John meant when he wrote "*God is love.*"[316] He didn't write it to assert that Yahweh's one and only facet is love; his point was that the totality of God's essence is love, whether or not it is always readily understood or obvious. The Bible clearly invokes other aspects of Yahweh's character that would be described as anything but love; at least from our perspective. So the fundamentalist mentality of extracting this single text to use as premise for a claim discounts many other characteristics and qualities of Yahweh, and is intellectually dishonest. John's scripture doesn't negate the others so much as sum them up. The God of our universe is not uni-dimensional, so to balance a doctrine with such far reaching implications as the Trinity on such a precariously fragile interpretation of scripture is pure folly.

My intention in this chapter was to give a brief glimpse into the development of this doctrine to shed some light on why it exists. The Trinity is not founded upon the beliefs of the first Christians or of Christ himself. This is evidenced by the 350 year lag between the time of Christ's death and its formal establishment within the Church. In that time, through the efforts of some zealous but misguided individuals, the monotheism espoused by Jesus was usurped by a triad of gods that runs contrary to everything for which scripture and Jesus taught. However, I feel that it really isn't important to explain *why* Trinitarians think the way they do. The fearless explorers who circumvented the globe didn't need to explain *why* their predecessors thought the world was flat; they simply proved that it was round. In the same fashion, this book, or, more importantly, the Bible, gives ample proof as to what Jesus taught and what his first followers believed. Jesus never taught the Trinity doctrine or anything remotely close to it; so *why* Trinitarians believe what they do is simply irrelevant.

The Emperor's New Clothes

If a doctrine is not unintelligible, it has to be vague; and if neither unintelligible nor vague, it has to be unverifiable.

Eric Hoffer[317]

Before wrapping it up, I want to give an example of the mindless rhetoric and double talk that runs rampant amidst otherwise thoughtful and intelligent individuals when they're asked to defend the Trinity doctrine. Having sat enthralled through many hours of his lectures and talks, I greatly admire much of what this sapient gentleman says and does. He is an inspiration to me in many ways. However, on this point he's mistaken and his very own words support my opinion. The contrast of his description of the Trinity against the rest of his body of work candidly exposes the major flaws found within the doctrine itself. For an orator as gifted as he, it's unfortunate that he cannot see his response for what it truly is: proof of its fallacy. If I come down too hard, it's only through sheer disappointment.

One the most gifted Christian intellectuals of our time, Ravi Zacharias, during a lecture at Penn State University in 2005, was asked to explain the Trinity in relation to the Law of Non-Contradiction, with the assertion being made that there cannot simultaneously be one god and three gods. [318] In his reply, this otherwise brilliant and articulate apologist was reduced to rambling a string of near incoherent non sequiturs, as he recalled the likes of C. S. Lewis, the Apostles, mathematicians, Mortimer Adler, Islam, love and the kitchen sink in a convoluted effort to explain this unexplainable doctrine. The nadir of Ravi's tortuous exegetical dance came with the proclamation that "the only way to explain unity and diversity in the effect is if you got unity and diversity in the first cause; and only in the Trinity is there unity and diversity in the community of the Trinity." This dizzying "explanation" left the bewildered audience more confused than when he began.

Ravi claimed that the writers of the gospels "were hard and purposeful in the reflection of what the doctrine of the Trinity is all about."[319]

They were?

How Ravi could know what they reflected upon is a mystery in itself. In any case, regardless of what he presumes they meant, the only "doctrine" that the writers actually put forth supported their God as defined in

Jewish scripture, and his messiah, whom God raised from the dead. Let's put this into the proper context. Jesus ushered in a new covenant described in Jeremiah that supplanted what had been the very core of Judaism-the Mosaic Law.[320] This would necessitate an explanation. Accordingly, there are at least fifteen chapters in the New Testament dedicated to changing the minds of Jewish converts regarding the Law. For instance, Paul spends a great deal of time trying to convince all who'll listen that, thanks to Jesus, circumcision has been abolished.[321] The Jerusalem Council, headed by James and Peter, also discussed the matter at great length before coming to the same conclusion.[322]

In contrast, there are none dedicated to changing their perspective on God. This is quite remarkable considering the implications. You have the Law handed down by God, and you have the very nature of the God himself. The position of the first Christians changed in regard to the Law and their writings reflect it. In the same respect, if the first Christians (who all were Jewish) had been convinced that their traditional concept of God had changed as dramatically as the Trinity supposes, they would have been sure to mention it. They didn't.

Ravi also claimed that the definitive answer for mankind's greatest search (the search for unity and diversity) is found in the Trinity. He stressed that understanding and appreciating this point is crucial to understanding the Trinity. What's interesting to note here is that in many times past Ravi has held that the greatest search was actually the search for truth. In fact, he said as much in a lecture entitled *Jesus Among Other Gods*, [323] referring to the question asked of Jesus by Pontus Pilate: *"What is truth?."*[324] Ravi even teamed forces with author

Os Guinness, theologian RC Sproul and others on a venture known as *The Truth Project* to answer, in Ravi's own words, "the single most important" and "greatest question."[325] However, on this occasion in Penn State Ravi insisted that man's greatest search has actually been for unity and diversity, which is effectively expressed in the Trinity. This makes perfect sense because it's one or the other: the Trinity or the truth.

At one point, Ravi rattled off several examples that he alleged correlated with the search for unity and diversity and, by extension, the Trinity: the ancient philosophic concept of quintessence or *fifth element*; the Latin phrase, E Pluribus Unum (out of many one) found on our American currency; and the word *university* itself. (The egg analogy is a little passé these days.)

Unfortunately Ravi, in a very rare moment of confusion, or perhaps, unconscious subterfuge, applied improper definitions to his examples, and then muddied ontology with semantics in order to make his point. First, quintessence was erroneously considered by the Greek philosophers to be another separate and distinct element, a fifth element alongside earth, water, fire and air. This element, also known as aether or ether, was once believed to make up the celestial bodies. It was not considered the essence that united the other four, as Ravi erroneously stated. Second, E Pluribus Unum refers to the thirteen colonies which became states in a new nation. It does not refer to thirteen sovereign nations that also simultaneously constitute a single nation. These newly formed states acknowledged the federal government as an entity separate and distinct from themselves, with powers that in many ways supplanted and even superseded their own. In no way does this mirror the Trinity doctrine. The same goes with the third example: the idea of a university.[326] Once again the goal is an aggregation establishing a singular new entity replete with its own agenda; a university is not a bunch of parts making up a single unit, which are each, nonetheless, equal to the unit that they establish. The creation of a new entity by subordinate parts does not constitute support for the Trinity but Ravi had to say something.

Tellingly, throughout his entire reply Ravi never once referred to scripture to support the concept. That's why analogies are used so profusely by Trinitarians. They avoid scripture and, if clever enough, are excellent distractions from fact. As homage to Trinitarians, I'll use my own analogy, albeit an admittedly factitious one. As the egg has historically been used by Trinitarians as an example of the Trinity (three-in-one i.e., yolk, albumen, shell) for the purposes of fairness and tradition I will use it for my analogy as well.

Something seems to magically occur to eggs when they number one more than eleven; they become an entirely new entity called *one dozen* (twelve-in-one, otherwise known as the *Egghead*). Without the safety and security that comes from the collective known as *one dozen,* the solitary egg is at the mercy of nature. However, this *one dozen*, through the symbiotic relationship of the twelve, transcends nature to create a mysterious property that binds, protects and unifies the twelve through the four dimensions of space and time. This property is casually known as a *carton*. Thus, we have on one level the unity and diversity of the Egghead i.e., the twelve-in-one. Yet, the true majesty of the unity and the diversity of *the one dozen* is expressed on a deeper level only when each egg transcends its uniqueness and merge together to reveal the wondrous creation known as the omelet. E Pluribus Unum!

My point, while admittedly farcical, is to show that every new relationship creates new dynamics so why stop at just three? For instance, Ravi mentioned C.S. Lewis' explanation of the three dimensions of space in reference to the Trinity. Loosely paraphrased he said that with each dimension in life you get new possibilities. With one dimension you get a line; with two you get a figure; and with three you get objects; these three dimensions, to Ravi and Lewis, correspond with the Godhead.

Wonderful!

Only why stop there?

Time is as equally important as the other three dimensions. After all, we can't exist without time; we're not static and neither is God or the universe. So why not add this crucial fourth dimension to their example? Because four dimensions don't jibe with their doctrine, that's why.

In reality, at best the examples given by Ravi only relate to the Trinity superficially, since the Trinity implies three coequal singular entities that, nonetheless, make up another single entity. At the end of nearly nine minutes, and an understandably dazed and confused audience, the question remained unanswered and the Law of Non-Contradiction stood. What's truly stunning is that Ravi believes that this clip best represents his explanation of the Trinity. He's actually touting it on his YouTube page: RZIM. Borrowing a phrase from Ravi himself, the closest he came to "unpacking the question" was his quoting Mortimer Adler's reasoning behind the existence of the Trinity doctrine: "There will have to be majesty and mystery in God himself…"[327]

It's a mystery alright.[328]

7 Final thoughts…

> *Can the ax boast greater power than the person who uses it? Is the saw greater than the person who saws? Can a rod strike unless a hand moves it? Can a wooden cane walk by itself?* Isaiah 10:15

We've covered a lot of ground together. Some of the material may, understandably, be difficult to absorb. For Christians who have been thoroughly, although unknowingly, indoctrinated by mainstream churches, the span from there to here will probably be too far to bridge. That's okay. Yahweh is patient, giving all the time in the world to approach him; nonetheless he still wants to be approached. Yahweh is also gracious; and he knows the heart of an individual. However, the truth is the truth whether or not it's believed or accepted. And, unfortunately, the majority of what's taught in Christian churches today simply isn't biblical; in other words it's not true. The Bible speaks frequently about having the proper spiritual foundation; without it the rest is futile. Modern Christianity is founded upon a slew of lies, the principal one being the Trinity. Steeped in centuries of man's political, economic, and personal agendas, the Christianity of today bears little resemblance to the message espoused by Jesus and his first followers. Much of what is preached as dogmatic gospel from modern pulpits has been insinuated into Christianity from pagan rituals, secular traditions, and men with unscrupulous intentions.

Once Christianity became the official state religion of the Empire, men flocked to it in droves.

However, the reasons why they did varied considerably from the early converts. Religious conviction became a distant third to the acquisition of fortune and power, which could be attained by professing faith in Christ. Amidst this convoluted confluence of false teachings and corrupt ambition grew the rapacious leviathan known as the Roman Catholic Church. This institution quickly became more of an all reaching political party than a religious institution. Whatever was expedient for the church's expansion of control over the masses, or its accumulation of wealth, was the chosen course. Whether or not a policy had anything to do with the true meaning of the gospel was irrelevant. The once pure and simple message of Jesus was replaced with a complicated web of deceit and misinformation intended to delude the masses into submission. An amalgamation of pertinent religious and philosophical persuasions was concocted in order to attract groups and individuals to the all-encompassing embrace of the Church. The Trinity doctrine was produced in this climate.

I've gone to great lengths to allow scripture to speak through this book in the effort to show that the Bible doesn't support the Trinity doctrine. In doing so it may appear that the ultimate problem of trying to prove a negative occurs, which, as fanatical lovers of Saharan unicorns know, trying to prove that something doesn't exist can be problematic to say the least. Sophisticated atheists on the debate circuit have long understood this. As a result, they have altered their argument from one of denying the existence of God, to that of arguing that there is no proof of the existence of God.

However, proving a negative is not the intention of this book. The point is showing that, by and large,

Christians do not practice their faith in alignment with Jesus and his early followers. I propose that there is an alternate way of being a Christian; one that more accurately reflects the practices of early Christians; one that better respects Yahweh, Jesus and the sacrifice that they made on the cross; one that is validated by scripture; one that, by its very essence, precludes the possibility of the Trinity.

If it seems that we spent a lot of time learning about the Hebrew Bible and Jewish history it is for this reason: Jesus wasn't Christian, he was Jewish, and so were all of his Apostles and early disciples. This important fact has been forgotten in all but a few churches. Early Christianity was a sect within Judaism, with Jesus paralleling Jewish tradition and fulfilling Jewish prophecies in a variety of ways. True, his actions replaced much for which Judaism stood, but Jesus didn't replace its God. This is evidenced by the effort devoted to changing the minds of Jews regarding their Mosaic Law. There are over a dozen chapters in the New Testament specifically written to amend their view of the Law. Yet there are none dedicated to changing their view of the very God who gave them the Law in the first place. In light of the dramatic, life altering shift the Trinity concept would have had on their theology, this is inexplicable. The Trinity would have necessitated explanation in excruciating detail to a people who had been worshipping their God in their way for centuries. The Bible is strangely silent on the matter.

Regrettably, many Jews didn't accept Jesus as their messiah. As a result Judaism has continued to be practiced in its traditional form right up to today. Equally regrettably, Christians have completely forgotten the point of Christ's ministry and resurrection by replacing Yahweh with Jesus. On the one hand we have Jews still waiting for the messiah to come, while on the other most Christians have replaced God with Jesus. Simply put, Jews have the right God and no savior; Christians have the right savior and no God.

My hope is to restore monotheism to Christianity, true monotheism, where Yahweh alone is supreme. This is the monotheism that Jesus taught and lived; one that was based on Jewish scripture. All of the New Testament authors accepted and asserted this as the basis of their writings. Not the fabricated, three-in-one pseudo-monotheism that's based on an elaborate union of carefully dissected scriptures, patched together to form the ungodly bulwark of false doctrine.

The insistence by Trinitarians to view scripture exclusively through the paradigm of the Trinity doesn't allow for much discussion. Scriptures are twisted and cajoled to fit the theory in such a manner that the theory becomes support for the scriptures rather than the other way around. In the process they become incoherent to all but the religious elite. To be sure, Trinitarians will emphatically try and refute the claim that the Trinity cannot be found in the Bible; and they will claim to rely on scripture. However, they can do so only with an extremely liberal interpretation of said scripture. In fact, the only way to find any evidence in the Bible for the Trinity is with the aid of another trinity: the Ouija board; the crystal ball; and the secret decoder ring. It doesn't hurt to suspend common sense and assume that the typical definitions of words somehow don't apply to the Bible. It also helps to believe that common words and phrases have somehow gained magical, esoteric definitions, which are only apparent and understandable by the sapient select few-the ones with the rings. You know the ones, the religious elite: the priests, the bishops, the elders, the rabbis, the reverends, the pastors, the annoying street preacher, the televangelist, etc., etc., etc.

The religious powers that be, Catholic or otherwise, have a vested financial interest in keeping the masses uninformed. Saving souls has become a distant second to balancing their budgets; and balancing their budgets depend entirely upon keeping the sheep around long enough to sheer them. And this, of course, is wholly dependent upon ensuring that the religious leaders and their institutions remain indispensable. What better way is there to accomplish this then to consistently assert that the Bible is far too complex for the layman to grasp? Or that there are certain truths contained within the Bible, such as the Trinity, that are only ascertained via the clergy? Where would these so-called men of god be if the masses actually understood that Jesus had replaced all of them, to a man?[329]

They all would be out of jobs.

The message in the Bible is very clear about this; thanks to God's generosity, we can now approach him directly.[330] However, this is not good for the business of religion. Accordingly, it is downplayed. We are taught in mainstream churches that the priesthood (church elite) is absolutely essential to the typical Christian; Jesus taught exactly the opposite. Jesus spent a good portion of his ministry berating the established church and religious leaders of his time and they despised him for it. The destruction of the Jewish Temple should have signaled the end to organized religion on any large scale. However, man, being rather ingenuitive, managed to replace the Jewish Temple and High Priest, with all of its pageantry and corrupt excesses, with a new temple and high priest even more pompous and fraudulent than the first. The Pope in all his splendorous glory sits on a throne in the Vatican surrounded by untold riches, while men bow before him to kiss his ring; a ring, incidentally, that if sold could feed a hungry village for several months. I don't remember this type of spectacle being displayed by the only true leader of our church. In fact, he did quite the opposite. He washed feet.

Jesus has become the access point to his Father. He is ground zero to God in the same way the temple of Yahweh was for the Jews until its final destruction by the Romans in the year 70. However, unlike the temple Christ's essence knows no geographical bounds. Christians dwell in the new temple of Yahweh wherever they happen to be. This is the reason Paul consistently wrote about being tied to Christ, or *in* Christ. Not only are we *in* God's temple, we are, in fact, *part* of God's temple wherever we are, together with Christ. In many ways the fall of the Jerusalem temple closed the final chapter on the old Mosaic covenant while helping to usher in the new way to approach Yahweh, through Jesus.[331] Yes, the new covenant began with Christ's resurrection, but the destruction of the temple, as prophesized by Jesus, drove the point home.[332] Devout Jews had been performing the same religious rituals and sacrifices in the same location as their forefathers for centuries. After Christ's crucifixion, but prior to the temple's destruction, many Christians still continued these sacred Jewish practices, which had been performed in the Jerusalem temple from time immemorial. We have to keep in mind that the vast majority of Christ's early followers were Jewish. These Jewish believers tried to wed their former religious customs with the message of salvation that came from Christ. This all came to an abrupt end with the fall of the temple. Forevermore Jesus would become the only way to approach God.

What Jesus didn't do was become the god of his disciples.

A good analogy would be that he became the lifeline to God. An even better one would be that God threw us a life preserver in the form of Jesus so that God could draw us back to himself. This is precisely what Paul believed as he wrote:

> *All of this is a gift from God, who brought us back to himself through Christ...We speak for Christ when we plead, "Come back to God!" For God made Christ, who never sinned, to be the offering for our sin so that we could be made right with God through Christ.*" 2nd Corinthians 5:18, 20-21

The examples from the scripture that started this chapter wonderfully illustrate the relationship between Yahweh and Jesus. Jesus was used as a tool by Yahweh to restore our relationship with Yahweh; not to restore our relationship with Jesus. Jesus constantly referred back to his Father on all matters, never once taking credit or asking anything from anyone else. This is where it gets difficult for many Christians because the cornerstone of modern Christianity is the belief that Jesus was a God on earth, or at the very least, is now a part of the Godhead. Nevertheless, scriptures do not support this belief. Peter and Paul both pointed out that Jesus is the cornerstone of

God's temple, not his own, and believers are stones of this temple right alongside him.[333] After his resurrection Jesus made a significant declaration to Mary Magdalene. He told her to "*go find my brothers and tell them that I am ascending to my Father and your Father, **to my God and your God.***"[334] He knew his place; it's unfortunate that most Christians don't. Let's briefly readdress the issue of Jesus being called god in the Bible.

Most Christians, including pastors, will argue until they're blue in the face that Jesus was called god quite often in the Bible; when they do they're inadvertently lumping together the many references to Yahweh with the few references to Jesus. Of the 3900 to nearly 4500 uses of the word in the Bible (depending on the translation), Jesus is called god only five or six times at best. To put this in its proper perspective, Moses, Aaron and Samuel were all called gods, and nearly as many times as Jesus. Are they all a part of a Godhead simply because they were called god at one time or another? Keep in mind that Moses and Aaron were called god by *the* God, by Yahweh himself. Being called god (Hebrew: *'elohim* or Greek: *theos*) in the Bible doesn't presuppose divinity. It definitely doesn't denote equality with Yahweh.

Now, let's talk about worshipping Jesus; or, rather, not worshipping him. Jesus never asked to be worshiped; none of the Apostles ever taught that he should be worshipped; and, no one in the Bible ever worshipped him. At least not in the same way they did for their God. There is a huge misunderstanding about this, stemming partly from the Greek word *proskuneo*, which was poorly translated in the King James Bible and then carried over into other translations, and partly from the

LORD/lord mix-up which we covered at the start of the book. The word *proskuneo,* which is typically translated in the KJV as *worship* actually means *to fawn or crouch* or *to prostrate oneself in homage* as defined in *The New Strong's Exhaustive Concordance of the Bible* is (G4352).[335] *Strong's* continues by saying the word is probably derived from two other Greek words *pros* (G4314), which denotes movement, direction or nearness, and *kuon* (G2965), which means dog; so a literal translation is *to lick like a dog.*

The word *proskuneo* didn't always have a religious connotation the way *worship* does in our language. It was often used to describe the act of bowing and begging. For instance, it was used to describe: a gentile woman who pleaded for Jesus to expel a demon from her daughter;[336] a ruler who begged Jesus to raise his dead daughter;[337] and a leper that wished to be cured.[338] It was also used by Jesus in his parable of the unforgiving debtor, in which a servant fell down before his master to beg for mercy.[339] Obviously, Jesus wasn't suggesting that the servant was rendering divine reverence to his master. He was actually groveling on his hands and knees.

However, there is a Greek word used in the Bible that specifically describes religious supplication or prayer and specifically in relation to God: *latreuo* (G3000). It is never used in any other context. *Latreuo* carries much more religious significance than *proskuneo*. How can we know this for sure? Jesus used it when rebuking Satan's demand to be worshipped like Yahweh. Notably, we can see the difference between *proskuneo* and *latreuo* in his response because Jesus used both in the same sentence: *"Get out of here, Satan," Jesus told him. "For the Scriptures say, 'You must worship [Yahweh] the LORD your God and serve only him.'"*[340] Here *proskuneo* is translated as *worship*, while *latreuo* is translated as *serve*. *Strong's* definition of *latreuo* is: *to minister to God, i.e. to render religious homage* to God. It was never used in any other manner. Keep in mind that Satan asked Jesus to kneel down *and* worship him, and Jesus covered both in his answer. One word is used to describe the physical act of kneeling and the other is used to describe the act of offering religious tribute to God. Unfortunately, most translations have them reversed. The more accurate translation of *proskuneo* in this sentence would be *bow down before*, while *worship* should have been used for *latreuo*.

By the way, Jesus was referencing Deuteronomy 6:13, so we know that he was deferring all religious worship to none other than Yahweh, himself. The writer of Hebrews confirmed this when he wrote: *"Christ offered himself to God as a perfect sacrifice for our sins... so that we can worship [latreuo] the living God;"*[341] and "*let us be thankful and please God by worshiping [latreuo] him with holy fear and awe.*"[342] Thanks to the blood of Jesus, Christians are now free to render religious homage to Yahweh. It doesn't say anything in the Bible about rendering religious homage to Jesus; in fact, Jesus even said not to do it. This is where the second issue gets drawn into the misunderstanding.

It is quite easy to assume that "the LORD" and "the Lord" are referring to the same person. To the uninformed the connection seems blatantly apparent. However, they refer to two separate beings: Yahweh and Jesus. If you recall, "the LORD" has actually been inserted into the Bible in place of God's name nearly 7000 times. The disrespect to our creator is undeniably obvious if we take into consideration a custom that is practiced innumerable times on a daily basis throughout the world. When people meet for the first time names are exchanged. This is not only polite, but extremely helpful in establishing a relationship, and with all future discourse. It's the first step towards getting to know each other. This is so obvious a practice it typically goes without saying. And to be sure that the importance of this wasn't lost the Bible was sure to mention it several times.

If a person or persons were assigned a particularly important task the Bible usually states that they were chosen by name; such as when David picked certain men "*by name*" to give thanks to Yahweh.[343] The Levitical priests were also all carefully "*listed by name*;"[344] and men were "*appointed by name*" to distribute, among other things, food to the Levites, the descendants of Aaron chosen to be temple priests.[345] This is pretty straight forward, though to some skeptics these scriptures might not mean too much. However, there are a few more scriptures that may.

Jesus said that he was called, "*by name*" by Yahweh while Jesus was still in Mary's womb.[346] Perhaps, more importantly, Jesus said that he would call "*his own sheep by name.*"[347] This kind of honor is the same that Yahweh gave to the Israelites. Yahweh equated knowing them "*by name*" with being his chosen people.[348] A short time later Isaiah explained that Yahweh "*rose up*" Cyrus, the king of Persia, for the sake of Israel; Yahweh called Cyrus "*by name*" to do his work.[349] Cyrus freed the Israelites from Babylonian captivity and allowed them to return to Jerusalem to rebuild the temple of Yahweh.

Finally, one of the greatest men of the Bible had the illustrious honor of being on a first name basis with God: *"[Yahweh said] to Moses, "I will indeed do what you have asked, for I look favorably on you, and I know you by name."*[350] Moses was well aware of this honor bestowed upon him. This knowledge, in fact, emboldened Moses to ask God to further reveal himself, which he gladly did: *"[Yahweh said], "I will make all my goodness pass before you, and I will call out my name, Yahweh, before you."*[351] Moses was one of the very few men in the Bible that was given the honor of having his name known by God. His reward was seeing God *and* hearing God say his own name, even though Moses already knew it. Keep in mind their first encounter where Yahweh called Moses by name, and then revealed to Moses his own name:

> *God also said to Moses, "Say this to the people of Israel:* ***Yahweh****, the God of your ancestors—the God of Abraham, the God of Isaac, and the God of Jacob—has sent me to you. This is my eternal name,* ***my name to remember for all generations****.*
>
> Exodus 3:15 (Emphasis added.)

This in itself should show the importance of God's name, let alone all of the dozens of other scriptures that demand his name be remembered and honored. Shouldn't we give the same kind of respect to God that God gives to his chosen flock? Or that we give to people we meet in our everyday life? By the fourth or fifth page of the Bible, we learn that people "*began to worship [Yahweh] by name*";[352] the practice began during the time of Adam and Eve's

grandson Enosh, which by all accounts was fairly early in man's history.
The last page of the Bible includes a mandate to *"worship only God."*[353] This injunction can be found in one respect or another in virtually every other Bible book, while worshipping anyone other than Yahweh being as equally forbidden. So we see that from Genesis to Revelation the one constant thread tying together all the books of the Bible is the need to worship Yahweh. If you have read to this point and still have doubts to the importance of God's name this scripture probably won't help … but it should. It's from the mouth of God:

> *[Yahweh] says, "I was ready to respond, but no one asked for help. I was ready to be found, but no one was looking for me. I said, 'Here I am, here I am!' to a nation that did not call on my name."* Isaiah 65:1

So why do we still have these mix-ups? The Dark Ages are over; the Bible has been translated into hundreds of languages; and the literacy rate has skyrocketed. So why do all of these unbiblical beliefs still persist in modern churches? For one, old habits die hard. Major denominations have had their doctrines in place for centuries, and they were put in place via the granddaddy of all denominations: the Roman Catholic Church, which created their doctrine via the Telephone Game over hundreds, if not thousands of years.

This once popular children's game, also known as Chinese Whispers, is excellent example of how a message can be distorted with repeated incantations and without returning to the original source of the information. For those unfamiliar, the game begins with children forming a circle. One child then whispers a secret message into the ear of the next child who does the same until the message has been passed around the circle. The original message is then compared to the message received by the last child. Invariably they are different from each other, sometimes greatly. This same principle has caused the original message of Jesus to be transformed into the mess we have today. Like a copy of a copy endlessly repeated through the centuries, the original has become all but lost under layers of human fingerprints and smudge marks.

A second reason has to do with the way Christians have been "coming to Christ" since the Reformation. Countless people have been "saved" through an emotional experience or crisis. These "Born Again" Christians then begin to attend one church or another, more for the experience than instruction. Studying what's actually in the Bible come much later, if at all. Many pastors have taken this exact route to the pulpit (feeling first and learning later) because they have been instructed by other preachers that were brought to Christ in precisely the same way. They in turn pass on what they've learned, the way they learned it, putting education second to emotional impact, with the message becoming distorted ever so slightly more, a 'la the Holy Telephone Game. As for the Catholic faith, very few people turn toward Catholicism on their own accord; it's more of a birthright than a choice. A Catholic person is born, not made. This is a good thing because the Catholic institution has strayed so far from the path it would be unrecognizable to Jesus or any of his early followers. It's ironic that they, more than any other denomination, hold to the tenet that the average man must rely on the priesthood to be a "true Christian."

The truth is the average pastor never learns much biblical history; and the Old Testament has practically become a footnote in modern churches. The first book that a person receives when attaching to a denomination with the intent of becoming a pastor is the denomination's doctrine. This has to be learned and embraced before anything else. The person never gets a chance to visit the desert island we spoke of at the start of this book; they never get the chance to just read the Bible without the influence of a denomination or another person's agenda. What *is* learned from the Bible comes primarily from the New Testament. Ironically, often times it is not Christ's message that's taught so much as it is Paul's. That's because to many churches Paul letters have become more important than the gospels of Jesus. This is beyond belief!

I'd like to close this book by noting that there have been great men of learning and understanding throughout history that have agreed with most or all of this book. These men had to fight the most powerful organization on earth, the Roman Catholic Church. Kings and queens would regularly pay homage to the Pope in order to receive a papal blessing; and refusal to obey the laws set by the Vatican would render one's soul to hell for all eternity. Unlike today, eternal damnation was not taken lightly. It took a strong will to put one's eternal soul on the line. It took conviction as equally resolute to allow oneself to be burned at the stake or flayed alive for disagreeing with the papacy. These were often the outcomes for men who defied the Church. This type of treatment continued after the Reformation, only under the banner of several different denominations instead of one. Even in the United States it wasn't until the 19th century that one could freely speak out against a major denomination and not feel the looming presence of reprisal over one's shoulder. Fortunately, it was in this new atmosphere of tolerance where one of the most gifted thinkers who ever lived took up the difficult task of addressing doctrinal problems pervading traditional religion.

Intellectual giant Thomas Jefferson, the man who penned the line: "Question with boldness even the existence of a God …" came to the same conclusions as we have in this book.[354] Evangelical author David Barton pointed out that Jefferson, and a large group of his contemporaries denied, among other things, the Trinity and the divinity of Jesus.[355] Known as the Restoration Movement, these Christians returned to the basics of Christ's teachings; in the process they removed quite a bit of the manmade doctrine which had infiltrated its way into Christianity over the years, including the idea of denominations. Pastors from across the spectrum who joined the movement simply referred to their congregations collectively as Christians. Curiously, Jefferson also favored a return to the gospels over the Epistles, actually going so far as denouncing Paul as the "first corruptor of the doctrines of Jesus."[356] Be that as it may, Jefferson and his peers were not alone in their views. For two thousand years men who have dared to challenge the powers that be and study the word on their own have come to the same conclusions found within this book. As I've said throughout this book, don't take my word on it. Get on an island and find out for yourself.

Acknowledgments

First and foremost, thank you Father for the life you have given me; and for allowing me to love others.

To my dear friend Dave, through whom God's love was first revealed to me. You touch more hearts then you can ever know, including mine. Thank you.

To my family at Clearview Christian Fellowship, thank you for allowing my family and me to be blessed with your love and kindness.

To my friends at the Monday Night Freedom NA group, thanks for helping me keep my head clear.

To my baby boy, Anthony, thank you for being the greatest child a dad could ever hope to have. You brought meaning to my life and more joy than I could have ever possibly imagined. I love you. No, I love you more!

To my wife, Cristiane, I want to say thank you for putting up with all of my many moods through these years; for loving me when I didn't deserve it; and for giving me the greatest gift I could ever receive, my son. I haven't said this often enough: I love you.

Most of all I want to thank you brother. You've supported everything I've ever done throughout my life, whether or not I knew, appreciated, accepted or deserved it. You have been my biggest fan. Without you this book would not have been written.

Thank you, Frank. I love you.

Finally, I want to thank you Maria for graciously taking time to edit this book. No if, and, or buts, this book has been greatly improved thanks to your meticulous efforts and wonderful suggestions. Thank you so very much.

About the Author

Anthony Fotia was born in Greenwich Connecticut in 1968. He helped found Clearview Christian Fellowship in Las Vegas in 2012. His goal is to restore Christianity to its former glory. He is self-educated.

Notes

---

[1] NKJV
[2] Luke 2:41-47
[3] Matthew 4:1-11
[4] Act 23:66
[5] 1st Kings 8:60; 2nd Chronicle 33:13; John 5:44; 1st Timothy 1:17; Jude 1:25
[6] Psalm 100:1-5; 1st Chronicles 16:25-31; Zechariah 8:20-22; Luke 4:8
[7] Genesis 4:26; Exodus 20:7; Joshua 9:18; Romans 10:13; 1st Chronicles 15:10; Act 2:21; Exodus 3:15
[8] Many Bible translations have substituted the phrase "the LORD" for the name Yahweh. Your Bible should give an explanation in its preface or introduction. A more detailed explanation of why this is so, as well as the reason we are using the name Yahweh over Jehovah, will be given in chapter two.
[9] John 10:36
[10] Matthew 4:10
[11] John 5:30, 6:38, 7:17
[12]Isaiah 44:3; Ezekiel 39:29; Joel 2:28
[13] Acts 2:17
[14] John 20:22
[15] Matthew 12:32; See also Luke 12:10 and Mark 3:28-29
[16] Ecclesiastes 1:5
[17] Psalm 104:5
[18] Joshua 10:12
[19] www.WorldChristianDatabase.org
[20] Whether or not the bull was valid is questionable since by the time of its delivery Leo had been dead three months.
[21] Center for the Study of Global Christianity (CSGC) at Gordon-Conwell Theological Seminary in South Hamilton, Mass. CSGC (This is the global sum of the total number of denominations in each country; so there is some overlap between countries.)
[22] John 20:17
[23] John 14:28
[24] The title of this song is taken directly from the Old Testament: Psalm 113:2 and Job 1:21.

---

[25] Acts 2:21 as quoted from Joel 2:32
[26] Exodus 20:2-3
[27] Genesis 12:3
[28] Joshua 8:33
[29] Alter, Robert. *The Five Books of Moses: A Translation with Commentary*. New York: W. W. Norton & Company, Inc., 2004. Print. p. 321
[30] Ibid. p. 321
[31] The 4th century Latin Vulgate incorrectly translated 'ehyeh' as *I AM*. Unfortunately, the Vulgate has been the foundation of many other translations, carrying the error through the centuries to our modern times. The result: *I AM* is incorrectly considered the name of God.
[32] Alter, Robert. *The Five Books of Moses: A Translation with Commentary*. New York: W. W. Norton & Company, Inc., 2004. Print. p. 321
[33] Ibid. p. 322
[34] Hebrew is actually read from right to left so the characters here are actually in reverse order from their natural spelling.
[35] Genesis 22:14; 1st Samuel 1:3; Psalm 23
[36] The temple was eventually rebuilt in 516 B.C.E. and stood for almost six centuries until it was destroyed again-this time by the Romans in 70 C. E. Thus Judaism began its transformation from a religion that revolved solely around their temple-and the sacrifices within it performed by the High Priest for atonement-into one that relied on rabbinical teachings in synagogues, and of atonement through good works.
[37] See also Isaiah 26:4 and 38:11.
[38] Alter, Robert. *The Book of Psalms: A Translation with Commentary*. New York: W. W. Norton & Company, Inc., 2007. Print. p. 396
[39] Matthew 22:44; Mark 12:36; Luke 20:42
[40] Act 2:34-35
[41] Acts 2:39
[42] Acts 13:47
[43] James 5:10-11
[44] 2nd Peter 2:9
[45] Luke 1:25
[46] Luke 1:15-16,19

[47] Luke 1:29-33
[48] Luke 1:68-69
[49] Acts 3:12-23
[50] Revelation 21:22
[51] Matthew 2:15; 8:17
[52] Matthew 9:38
[53] Luke 20:37; see Exodus 3:6
[54] Matthew 1:20, 2:19, 28:2; Luke 1:11; Acts 5:19, 8:26, 12:7, 11; compare to Zechariah 1:12-13 and Judges 2:4
[55] Acts 5:9, 8:39; compare to Ezekiel 37:1, 1st and Samuel 16:14
[56] James 5:4; compare to Isaiah 51:15 and Jeremiah 2:19
[57] Revelation 1:8, 18:8, 22:6; compare to Psalm 72:18 and Isaiah 26:4
[58] Isaiah 9:6
[59] Although *'elohim* is actually the plural form of *'el*, it is almost always used in the singular.
[60] Genesis 20:13Ibid. p. 100
[61] Genesis 23:6 Ibid. p. 114
[62] Exodus 4:16
[63] Exodus 7:1Ibid. p. 345
[64] Exodus 12:12
[65] Exodus 33:4
[66] 1st Samuel 28:13
[67] Psalm 82
[68] John 10:34
[69] 2nd Corinthians 4:4
[70] Jesus is the English version of the Hebrew name Yashua, which is also where we get, among other names, Joshua. Although the name Jesus is found in one form or another in the Old Testament it is not used there to denote the messiah. Incidentally, Yashua (pronounced '*yah shoo ah*') means *Yahweh is salvation.*
[71] Matthew 4
[72] Matthew 23:10
[73] The spelling variant stems yet again from the efforts of Jewish priests to keep the name *Yahweh* and its variation *Yah* holy. They transcribed *Yah* to *Yeh* to prevent its misuse whenever the name was read aloud. This change carried over to the pronunciation, and thus, the spelling of Jesus' name.
[74] Philippians 2:9

---

[75] Some suggest the correct pronunciation of Christ's name in Hebrew is Yeshu, thereby delineating a separation between Jesus' name and other names within the Old Testament, but there is simply no sound archaeological, or textual evidence to support this theory. Yeshu is found only in rabbinic writings penned long after the time Christ lived.
[76] Isaiah 45:1
[77] There are non-Christian historical sources outside of the Bible, which support the biblical story of Jesus; Josephus, Tacitus and Pliny the Younger are just a few men whose writings confirm the existence of Jesus, and of his early followers. That Jesus walked the earth, had religious devotees, was said to have performed miracles and was crucified is not in question by reputable scholars.
[78] Acts 1:4-8
[79] Acts 9:3-16
[80] As a part of Saul's conversion Jesus also visited a disciple named Ananias in a vision. Ananias found Saul, restored his sight and filled him with God's spirit.
[81] John does give a brief, poetic synapsis of Jesus' life in heaven with Yahweh at the gospel's start.
[82] Luke 2:49
[83] John 4:34, 6:29, 6:46, 6:57
[84] John 8:38, 40
[85] John 17:5
[86] John 16:28
[87] Hebrews 1:2; Colossians 1:16
[88] Hebrews 1:6; Colossians 1:15
[89] John 6:27
[90] Matthew 3:16-17; Mark 1:10-11; Luke 3:22
[91] John 1:32-35
[92] John 3:34-35
[93] Luke 3:23
[94] These various prophecies were recorded on individual scrolls, which were eventually combined with the five books of Moses, otherwise known as the Torah, and several other scrolls known collectively as the wisdom books, to become the Jewish Holy Bible.
[95] Even today people of Jewish faith are still waiting for his arrival, as they don't consider Jesus to be the true messiah.
[96] Isaiah 61:1-2 (See Luke 4:16-21)

[97] Luke 4:21
[98] Matthew 21:42; Mark 12:10-11; Luke 20:17
[99] Matthew 16:15-17; See also Mark 8:29
[100] Matthew 23:10
[101] John 5:39
[102] Matthew 22:41-45, Mark 12:35-37; Luke 20:41-44 (As we learned earlier, God's name has been replaced by "the LORD" in these and many other scriptures.)
[103] John 44:26
[104] John 8:48
[105] John 4:20
[106] Matthew 26:64
[107] The Jewish leaders had an additional reason to have Jesus executed-their jobs were at stake. Jesus had been preaching against the Jewish establishment with all of its man-made rituals. He railed against the corruption and hypocrisy among the so-called religious elite. He also taught that it would no longer be necessary to approach Yahweh through the priesthood. Jesus himself would be the high priest for all of his followers, sidestepping the established order.
[108] Matthew 24:5, 23; Mark 13:5, 21-22 and Luke 21:8
[109] John 5:36; 10:25
[110] Matthew 18:10; John 5:17 and Luke 2:49
[111] John 6:46 and John 5:28
[112] 1st Kings 5:5
[113] Matthew 16:15-16
[114] Matthew 17:1-9, Mark 9:2-9; Luke 9:28-36
[115] Matthew 17:5
[116] Mark 5:7
[117] Luke 4:34
[118] Luke 4:41
[119] Matthew 26:64; Mark 14:62; Luke 22:70 (The NKJV translates his response in Luke as "*you rightly say that I am.*")
[120] Job 2:1, 38:7; Matthew 5:9; Luke 20:36; Roman 8:14, 19; Galatians 3:26
[121] Daniel 7
[122] John 10:30
[123] John 10:38; John 14:7; John 16:32
[124] Matthew 10:34
[125] Matthew 10:16

---

[126] Luke 8:10
[127] Mark 8:33; Matthew 15:24; Matthew 24:8; Luke 5:10; Mark 8:34
[128] Matthew 5:48; Mark 11:25; Matthew 10:40; Mark 9:37; John 5:23; John 16:28; John 8:17-18
[129] John 14:1
[130] Matthew 11:25-26; Mark 7:34; John 17:15; Mark 14:32; Luke 22:42
[131] Luke 11:41-42
[132] Luke 22:32
[133] Matthew 27:46; Mark 15:34
[134] Matthew 3:17; Mark 1:11; Luke 3:22; Matthew 17:5; Mark 9:7
[135] John 1:32-34
[136] 2nd Peter 1:16-17
[137] The two instances to which I refer are the destruction of the two cities of Sodom and Gomorrah, and the flood in which only Noah and his family survived. Yahweh also angrily told Moses that he wanted to wipe out the recalcitrant Israelites and start over with Moses and his family. Fortunately for the Israelites, Moses was able to convince God to spare them.
[138] Matthew 11:25
[139] Psalm 119:130
[140] Isaiah 29:13
[141] Mark 7:6-8
[142] Hebrew 7:1-28
[143] 1st Peter 2:5
[144] John 14:26
[145] John 10:30; 10:38; 14:7; 16:32
[146] Matthew 19:3
[147] One final note on John 10:30, if Jesus was really trying to show that he and his Father were one and the same, wouldn't it have made better sense if he said "the Father and I *am* one," instead of "*are* one?" Put another way, is Jesus saying 'I *am* my Father' or 'I *are* my Father?' Besides being a singular verb, which would have made better sense if they were the same being, using *am* would have tied together nicely with the popular, albeit misrepresented, designation for Jesus-I AM
[148] Deuteronomy 4:39
[149] Isaiah 43:10
[150] Mark 12:29-30

---

[151] Deuteronomy 6:4-5
[152] Deuteronomy 6:13, 16
[153] John 14:28
[154] Mark 10:45
[155] Matthew 4:10
[156] John 6:38
[157] John 18:11
[158] Matthew 26:39, 42 (See also Mark 14:36, 39 and Luke 22:42)
[159] See also John 5:37; 7:16, 29, 33; 8:26; Luke 9:47; 10:16; 11:30
[160] Luke 18:19 (See also Matthew 19:17 and Mark 10:18)
[161] Hebrews 7:26
[162] John 5:26; Acts 10:38
[163] Matthew 10:5-8, 28:18-20; Luke 10:1-9; John 17:18
[164] Matthew 9:4, Mark 2:10, Luke 5:24
[165] John 5:22; 5:27; Matthew 16:27
[166] John 5:30
[167] Matthew 24:36 (see also Mark 13:32)
[168] Matthew 20:23 (see also Mark 10:40)
[169] Colossians 1:15
[170] Hebrews 1:5-6
[171] Psalm 89:27
[172] John 6:57
[173] Luke 23:46
[174] John 14:28
[175] Matthew 26:64; Mark 14:62; Luke 22:69
[176] John 20:17
[177] John 10:7
[178] John 10; Matthew 25:32
[179] Zechariah 13:7
[180] Psalm 23:1 (NKJV)
[181] This is known as the fallacy of composition.
[182] Psalm 49:14
[183] Ezekiel 34:11-12
[184] Ezekiel 34:13-23
[185] John 10:14-15
[186] Mark 14:27 (Quoting from Zechariah 13:7)
[187] Acts 20:28
[188] 1st Peter 5:2
[189] John 10:7, 9

[190] Isaiah 43:11
[191] John 14:6
[192] Leviticus 23:28 (Jews still observe it to this day, although the procedure has been changed since the destruction of the temple in 70 A.D.)
[193] Psalm 110:1
[194] Exodus 12
[195] Luke 22:19-20
[196] Luke 23:13
[197] Hebrews 9:14
[198] John 19:33
[199] John 19:34
[200] Luke 23:53-54
[201] Hebrews 9
[202] John 1:51
[203] John 14:6
[204] John 15:1, 5
[205] Psalm 45:7 (Emphasis added.)
[206] See also John 20:17
[207] There have been major textual discoveries, such as the Dead Sea Scrolls, as well as major advances in the field of linguistics in relation to biblical languages since the writing of the King James Bible. While the poetic style has become engrained in our Christian culture, to believe that this archaic version represents the best we have for comprehension borders on the absurd.
[208] Revelation 1:8 (NLT)
[209] Revelation 21:6-7
[210] John 19:30
[211] Revelation 22:1-5
[212] Revelation 22:6
[213] Revelation 22:12-13
[214] For those unfamiliar with red letter Bibles, many Bibles are called red letter editions because wherever Jesus is supposedly being quoted the text is printed in red letters.
[215] Exodus 3:14
[216] John 8:58
[217] We learned in chapter 2, the most probable meaning of the Hebrew word *Ehyeh* is *I will be.* Thus the most plausible translation of the phrase in question is *I will be who I will be.*

[218] Mark 14:61-62
[219] A certain Bible translation also refers to Jesus as god in John 1:18, and in 2nd Peter 1:1. However, this is not the view held by the majority of translations so I don't consider them worth counting. Nevertheless, they will each be addressed in the chapter on the Apostles.
[220] Matthew 15:9
[221] Matthew 11:25-26
[222] John 1:2
[223] John 20:28
[224] John 10:34-36
[225] Matthew 16:16
[226] See also Mark 8:27-29
[227] John 20:17
[228] John 14:26, 15:12, 16:7
[229] Matthew 3:16; Mark 1:10; Luke 3:22; John 1:32
[230] Genesis 4:7
[231] Jeremiah 15:13
[232] Psalm 36:1
[233] Isaiah 59:4
[234] Romans 6 and 7
[235] Job 21:20
[236] For those keeping track – in addition to the above verses we find God's wrath being poured out in 2nd Chronicles 34:21, 25; Isaiah 42:25, 51:20; Lamentations 2:4, 4:11; Ezekiel 22:22, 36:18; and Zephaniah 1:15 just to name a few.
[237] Jeremiah 25:15-17, 26-28
[238] Jeremiah 48:21; Daniel 9:27; Psalm 85:1; Psalm 22:14; 2nd Timothy 4:6; Ephesians 1:6; 1st Corinthians 15:10; Lamentations 2:11; Ezekiel 16:36
[239] Proverbs 1:23, 33
[240] Proverbs 1:33, 3:13, 3:18, 4:6, 3:16, 4:8
[241] Proverbs 2:12, 16
[242] Proverbs 9:4-6
[243] Proverbs 1:20
[244] Ecclesiastes 7:24
[245] Proverbs 4:8, 7:4
[246] Exodus 28:3, 36:1 (See also Exodus 31:3 and 35:31)
[247] Deuteronomy 34:9

---

[248] 1st Corinthians 2:7
[249] 1st Corinthians 1:17
[250] Matthew 11:19 (See also Luke 7:35)
[251] Luke 2:40
[252] James 3:17
[253] Proverbs 3:18
[254] Proverbs 3:19
[255] Pagels, Elaine. *The Gnostic Gospels.* New York: Vintage Books, 1989. Print. p.124
[256] Acts 6:3
[257] Acts 6:10 (Emphasis added.)
[258] Isaiah 19:14
[259] Ezekiel 23:8
[260] 2nd Timothy 1:7
[261] Isaiah 57:15
[262] The phrase *holy spirit* or, more precisely, *spirit of holiness* is found just three times in the Old Testament: Psalm 55:11; Isaiah 63:10 and11; none of which refer to an actual deity.
[263] John 3:6
[264] 1st Corinthians 1:10; Philippians 2:1-2; 1st Peter 3:8
[265] Matthew 3:16
[266] Acts 8:17-23
[267] Acts 21:11
[268] Acts 3:6-8
[269] Acts 20:9-10
[270] Isaiah 32:15
[271] Micah 3:8
[272] Acts 10:45
[273] Titus 3:5-6
[274] Ephesians 5:18
[275] 1st Corinthians 12:13 NKJV
[276] Genesis 2:7
[277] John 20:22
[278] Acts 10:47; 15:8 (Compare to Acts 2:2)
[279] Mark 5:24-34
[280] Mark 3:28-29
[281] Matthew 12:31
[282] This analogy was actually used by a radio preacher whose name, unfortunately escapes me. He tried to explain away Deuteronomy

6:4: *"Hear, O Israel: The Lord our God, the Lord is one!"* (NKJV)
[283] Hoffer, Eric. *The True Believer: Thoughts on the Nature of Mass Movements*. New York: HarperCollins Publishers, Inc., 2002. Print. p.81
[284] I use the term God here in its current sense, i.e. as an equal person in the Godhead. Recall that the Hebrew term *'elohim*, translated as *god* was used in a variety of contexts; as did the Greek *theos.*
[285] Actually even this is a misnomer because the Eastern and Western Orthodox Churches never really came to a consensus on the Trinity. To this day their doctrines differ from each other.
[286] Ehrman, Bart D. *Misquoting Jesus: The Story Behind Who Changed the Bible and Why*. New York: HarperCollins Publishers, Inc., 2005. Print. pp. 81-82
[287] 1st John 5:7 (NKJV)
[288] Armstrong, Karen. *A History of God: The 4,000 – year quest of Judaism, Christianity and Islam*. New York: Random House Inc., 1993. Print. p. 117
[289] Genesis 6:1 (NKJV)
[290] As a continuance to Mary's alleged divinity, the Catholic doctrine of the Immaculate Conception was concocted to explain how Mary could give birth to Jesus if she was contaminated by original sin. The doctrine, officially formalized in 1854 by Pope Pius IX, reverse engineered Mary's birth and declared that she herself was born sinless, thus, solving the problem.
[291] Acts 14:11-13
[292] Ehrman, Bart D. *How Jesus Became God: The Exaltation of a Jewish Preacher from Galilee*. New York: HarperCollins Publishers, 2014. Print. pp. 21-22
[293] John 14:12
[294] Among their many miracles, both Peter and Paul raised people from the dead. And while the Bible implies that Peter's shadow was able to heal the sick there is no reference of this happening from the shadow of Jesus. (See Acts 5:15, 9:40, 20:10)
[295] Luke 23:46
[296] Ephesians 2:4-6
[297] Matthew 27:51-53
[298] Kirby, Peter. "Martyrdom of Polycarp." *Early Christian Writings*. 2013. 1 Oct. 2013 <http://www.earlychristianwritings.com/martyrdompolycarp.html>.

Chapter 20:2

[299] Kirby, Peter. "Justin Martyr." *Early Christian Writings*. 2013. 1 Oct. 2013 <http://www.earlychristianwritings.com/justin.html>. Chapter 22

[300] Ibid. Chapter 6

[301] Kirby, Peter. "Tatian's Address to the Greeks." *Early Christian Writings*. 2013. 1 Oct. 2013 <http://www.earlychristianwritings.com/tatian.html>. Chapter 5

[302] Kirby, Peter. "Irenaeus of Lyons." *Early Christian Writings*. 2013. 1 Oct. 2013 <http://www.earlychristianwritings.com/irenaeus.html>. *Against Heresies.* Book 1 Chapter 28:1

[303] Ibid.

[304] Kirby, Peter. "Origen." *Early Christian Writings*. 2013. 1 Oct. 2013 <http://www.earlychristianwritings.com/origen.html>. Book 2 Chapter 2 (Compare with Colossians 1:15-16)

[305] See also Revelations 1:5

[306] Revelation 3:14 (NKJV)

[307] Luke 7:12, 8:42, 9:38

[308] Hebrews 11:17 (See Genesis 21:12)

[309] Genesis 22:12

[310] Hebrews 11:28

[311] Hebrews 12:16

[312]Armstrong, Karen. *A History of God: The 4,000 – year quest of Judaism, Christianity and Islam*. New York: Random House Inc., 1993. Print. p. 111

[313] Hammond, Gerald, and Austin Busch. *The English Bible King James Version: The New Testament and The Apocrypha*. New York: W.W. Norton & Company, Inc., 2012. Print. p. xxiv

[314] As throughout this book, for our purposes the term Trinity is interchangeable with Godhead and Triune. All denote the same basic polytheistic three-gods-in-one doctrine.

[315] Anyone interested in uncovering the truth about Darwinism and the biasness of the evolutionist community in interpreting findings across all fields of science should read Phillip E. Johnson's book, *Darwin on Trial.*

[316] 1st John 4:8

[317] Hoffer, Eric. *The True Believer: Thoughts on the Nature of Mass Movements*. New York: HarperCollins Publishers, Inc., 2002. Print. p. 81

[318] The video clip can be found on the YouTube channel *Ravi Zacharias International Ministries* under the heading: *The Law of Non-Contradiction and the Trinity.* https://www.youtube.com/watch?v=kreSbagj_RM
[319] Ibid.
[320] Jeremiah 31:31-34
[321] Galatians 5:1-12
[322] Acts 15:1-21
[323] This lecture can found on YouTube under the heading: *Jesus Among Other Gods – Ravi Zacharias.* https://www.youtube.com/watch?v=eaIBoARTGPk
[324] John 18:38
[325] Ravi is quoted from the YouTube video clip: *What is truth? Ravi Zacharias, OS Guinness, RC Sproul.* https://www.youtube.com/watch?v=9AARDtGay5w See also www.thetruthproject.org
[326] I'm going to assume that Ravi was trying to use the concept of a university for his example, even though he said that the word "defined" is unity and diversity. Just in case he actually made such a basic etymological error I will clarify: university is derived from the Latin: *uni* (one) and *versus* (turn), i.e. *turn into one*. It is not the melding of the words *unity* and *diversity,* as he implied.
[327] Ibid.
[328] The author contacted the office of Dr. Zacharias at which time I spoke with his assistant Priscilla David. My requests for further comments went unanswered. Emails confirm that Dr. Zacharias stands by his afore mentioned statements.
[329] Matthew 23:8-12
[330] Isaiah 49:6; Hebrews 4-9
[331] John 14:6
[332] Matthew 24:2 (Jews were given yet an additional sign that the temple had become obsolete in the 2nd century when they were completely barred from the city of Jerusalem by the Romans. As a final insult, the Romans renamed the town Palestine after the Philistines, the main enemy of the Jews in their Bible.)
[333] 2nd Corinthians 6:16; 1st Peter 2:4-5
[334] John 20:17 (Emphasis added.)
[335] Strong, James. *The New Strong's Exhaustive Concordance of the Bible*. Nashville: Thomas Nelson, Inc., 1990. Print. (*The New*

Strong's Exhaustive Concordance of the Bible is the most accepted Hebrew to English, and Greek to English dictionary available. It is *the* bible of Bible words. Each word is conveniently designated with a letter, H for Hebrew and G for Greek, followed by a four digit number, which are listed numerically in their respective languages.)

[336] Matthew 15:25

[337] Matthew 9:18

[338] Matthew 8:2

[339] Matthew 18:26

[340] Matthew 4:10

[341] Hebrews 9:14

[342] Hebrews 12:28

[343] 1st Chronicles 16:41

[344] Ezra 8:20

[345] 2nd Chronicles 31:19

[346] Isaiah 49:1

[347] John 10:3

[348] Isaiah 43:1

[349] Isaiah 45:3

[350] Exodus 33:17

[351] Exodus 33:19

[352] Genesis 4:26

[353] Revelation 22:9

[354] Contrary to popular opinion, this oft misrepresented line from Jefferson was actually an appeal to his nephew Peter Carr to be able to defend his position about God; Jefferson was in no way personally doubting his existence. A careful study of his writings shows a man passionate about religion in general and Christ specifically.

[355] Barton, David. *The Jefferson Lies: Exposing the myths you've always believed about Thomas Jefferson.* Nashville: Thomas Nelson, Inc., 2012. Print. p. 184

[356] Ibid. p. 180

Made in the USA
San Bernardino, CA
08 August 2017